Your Daily Journey to
Transformation

Also by Jim Ayer

Second Chance
Transformation
Remodeling Your Life DVD series

To order, call **1-800-765-6955.**

Your Daily Journey to

Transformation

Jim Ayer with Janene Ayer

REVIEW AND HERALD® PUBLISHING ASSOCIATION

Since 1861 | www.reviewandherald.com

The Review and Herald® Publishing Association publishes biblically based materials for spiritual, physical, and mental growth and Christian discipleship.

Statements in this volume attributed to other speakers/writers are included for the value of the individual statements only. No endorsement of those speakers'/writers' other works or statements is intended or implied.

Unless otherwise noted, all Scripture references are taken from the New King James Version. Copyright © 1982 by Thomas Nelson, Inc. Used by permission.

Scriptures credited to ICB are quoted from the *International Children's Bible, New Century Version,* copyright © 1983, 1986, 1988 by Word Publishing, Dallas, Texas 75039. Used by permission.

Bible texts credited to TEV are from the *Good News Bible*—Old Testament: Copyright © American Bible Society 1976, 1992; New Testament: Copyright © American Bible Society 1966, 1971, 1976, 1992.

This book was
Edited by Anthony Lester
Copyedited by Delma Miller
Designed by Derek Knecht/Review & Herald® Design Center
Cover design by David Berthiaume
Typeset: Minion Pro

PRINTED IN U.S.A.
March 2015

Library of Congress Cataloging-in-Publication Data

Ayer, Jim, 1948-   .
   Your daily journey to transformation: a study guide/Jim and Janene Ayer.
      p. cm.

1. Christian life. I. Title.
BV4501.3.A955 2013
248.4'86732—dc23
A976
ISBN 978-0-8280-2702-1   2012049327

Contents

About Jim Ayer

Jim Ayer is the host of the popular television series *Making Waves,* which is broadcast on 15 networks all around the world. As an international speaker, Jim focuses on how to form a genuine, committed relationship with God, whose desire is to revive and transform us into His image so that we can be joint heirs to heaven's glory. He has written numerous articles and books, including his personal story, *Second Chance*, and his latest book, *Transformation*.

About Janene Ayer

Janene Ayer is an entrepreneur, real-estate broker, loving mother, and a very proud grandmother of three bright grandchildren. In addition, she breeds, trains, and sells Morgan horses, but her greatest love is found in fellowship with her Best Friend—Jesus Christ. It is her desire and burden to have everyone experience the same joy of fellowship she has discovered.

A Note From the Author

I highly recommend reading my book *Transformation*. It contains many additional spiritual insights that will help you to behold the Lamb of God and will aid you in your transformation journey! To order, call 1-800-765-6955.

Preface

Martin Luther King, Jr., had it right. He said, "Take the first step in faith. You don't have to see the whole staircase, just take the first step."

Unfortunately, most of us spend more time planning for our next vacation than we do taking the first step of faith in our pursuit of heaven. At times we can even seem paralyzed in our spiritual walk.

There was a time in my life that the words "growing in Jesus" were not part of my vocabulary; the idea of overcoming sin held little attraction for me. Had I been completely honest with myself at that time, I could have said, "I have not made a 100 percent commitment to Jesus. I'm not going to make it to heaven like this!"

But that all changed the day God offered me a second chance, inviting me to join Him on an exciting new journey. He brought me to the crossroads of life and death. I confessed to Him that although I was a tithe-paying, nicely dressed church member in good standing, I was lost. The day I made the choice to accept Christ's invitation and took that first step up the ladder to heaven, I began to experience an amazing life transformation!

Now, what about you? Please take a few moments for your own self-assessment . . . and it's crucial that you are completely honest with yourself and with God!

How is your relationship with the Lord? Does He come first in everything in your life?

Can you say—without a doubt—that you have been growing in your friendship with Jesus?

Do you have complete assurance that if Jesus returned today, you would be excited about His return? Would you be ready to go home with Him?

Is your walk on life's pathway making Jesus happy, or are you regularly causing Him pain by yielding to every temptation? Does repeated sin in your life cause you anguish and regret while leaving you feeling helpless to do anything about it?

If you desire more from your Christian experience than what you now have, **act upon that desire immediately!** Seize eternal life and hang on—you are in for an amazing journey!

"If you don't go after what you want, you'll never have it. If you don't ask, the answer is always no. If you don't step forward, you're always in the same place."—Nora Roberts.

The devil will tell you, "You should be anxious and wary about 'change.' Don't get involved; don't become radical— you're just fine the way you are. If you act in haste, you might lose something that's very dear to you."

But God is inviting you to join me on the journey of a lifetime through this study guide. He is a wonderful and loving guide who has planned a glorious future for you, and as soon as you take the first few steps, you will wonder why you didn't start sooner!

Please fill in the date below. Once you start the journey, you will look back on this moment knowing just when it was that you took the first steps on the pathway of eternal life—when the start of a relationship with Christ that once seemed out of reach first began.

Today's Date: _____, _____

Wishing you many blessings, fellow traveler,
Jim Ayer

Your Daily Journey to Transformation Commitment

I'm not the type of person who likes to sign covenants or commit to anything that I might not follow through on. Yet many years ago I was faced with signing the commitment page of a study guide that was destined to change my life. I look back on that moment and shudder to think that I almost didn't do it!

Had I failed to commit at that time, I might not be urging you today to join me in this journey of eternity. You see, those are the stakes—eternity. Please do yourself and those you love a favor and sign now. You will be so glad you did!

My Personal and Group Covenant

I covenant with my *Your Daily Journey to Transformation* group to do the following:

1. To complete the weekly workbook lessons prior to meeting with my group

2. To lift up my group members in prayer each day, asking that each one will experience the transformational power of the Holy Spirit

3. To keep confidential all matters of a sensitive nature that any group member might share

4. To discover at least one thing for which to thank God each day . . . and do it!

Signed _____ Date_____ , _____

1

Celestial Plan

ohn the Baptist was standing on the muddy bank of the Jordan River when, seeing Jesus, he called everyone's attention to the One who was the object of his labor: "Behold! The Lamb of God who takes away the sin of the world!" (John 1:29). Now fast-forward to the judgment hall of Pontius Pilate, where attention is again called to Jesus: "Then Jesus came out, wearing the crown of thorns and the purple robe. And Pilate said to them, 'Behold the Man!'" (John 19:5).

Strong's Concordance defines the word "behold," as understood in the Greek, as "to gaze (i.e., with wide-open eyes, as at something remarkable)."

I have a friend who conducted an outreach training school for many years. Often when watching young people in the field preaching, I could actually pick out the ones who had attended his school. You see, my friend was such a magnetic and powerful evangelist and teacher that everyone who went through his course couldn't help mimicking his style. The more time they spent watching him, the more they became him in the pulpit.

This week, and for the rest of your time in this guide, spend as much time as you can with your eyes fixed upon Christ. This is key to your transformation. *"As you behold Him, you will be charmed with the riches of the glory of His divine love"* (*Review and Herald*, June 23, 1896). *"Self will sink into insignificance, and you will be changed into His image, 'from glory to glory, even as by the Spirit of the Lord'"* (*Youth's Instructor*, Sept. 9, 1897).

As you now move on to **Day 1**, to gaze "with wide-open eyes, as at something remarkable," prepare your heart by saying this prayer:

"Lord, help me not to be distracted while I study with You today, so that I can fully behold You. Give me a depth of understanding into Your love to a degree that I have not yet experienced! When this week has passed, may I be closer to You than ever before! I ask this in the beautiful and powerful name of Jesus."

God's Counterpart

"Men shall speak of the might of Your awesome
acts, and I will declare Your greatness."
—Psalm 145:6

Because my name, Jim Ayer, is nearly identical to that of Jim Ayars—formally the bass singer for the King's Heralds Quartet—I'm always being mistaken for him. That's just fine with me, since he sings better than I do and is much better looking than I am!

He also loves to study genealogy, so I once sent him my family history going back to within 20 years of the Pilgrims' first landing in America. It's all contained in an old book that my mom and dad handed down to me years ago. After Jim did a little more sleuthing, he discovered that, sure enough, even though our names are spelled differently, we were all one family in England back in the fifteenth century.

What made his findings all the more interesting is that we apparently still have a family *castle* in England. Wow! We have royal blood flowing through our veins. (It's only a tiny bit, sure, but it's still royal!) However, our family history is only a drop in the bucket when compared to another book that contains the genealogy of humanity itself . . .

"God said, 'Let Us make man in Our image, according to Our likeness'" (Gen. 1:26).

"Behold what manner of love the Father has bestowed on us, that we should be called children of God!" (1 John 3:1). There it is—royal blood coursing through not only my veins, but *yours, too!* You and I were created to be children of the King!

You are so special to God! What are your feelings at this moment, knowing that you were created to be royalty? Check each box that applies to you:

☐ I don't feel very special.
☐ It's hard to imagine that God cares that much for me.
☐ I want to believe.
☐ I do believe that I am very special to God.
☐ Other: _____

Explain your choice:

_____

_____

Additional Insight

*"Man was the crowning act of the creation of God, made in the image of God,
and designed to be a counterpart of God. . . . Man is very dear to God, because
he was formed in his own image"* (*Review and Herald,* June 18, 1895).

Ponder the definition of "counterpart," realizing that God has planned this as your ultimate destiny:

- one that closely resembles another
- one that has the same functions and characteristics as another
- one of two parts that fit and complete each other

"God created man a superior being; he alone is formed in the image of God, and is capable of partaking of the divine nature, of cooperating with his Creator and executing His plans" (Sons and Daughters of God, p. 7).

Bearing in mind the vastness of God's creation, describe how you feel at this moment, knowing you are destined to be a **partaker of the divine nature:**

_____
_____
_____

Consider God's plan for you:

- You were the crowning act of God's creative power.
- You were designed as a counterpart to God.
- You were formed in God's own image.

Yes! God has a plan for your life. Are you aware of what that plan is? If you don't know, share those thoughts here also . . .

_____
_____
_____

➡ **Taking time with the Lord.** Share your thoughts and feelings with Him in prayer. What is going on inside of you at this moment? He'll be happy to talk with you regardless of what your thoughts might be.

> *"Men shall speak of the might of Your awesome acts,*
> *and I will declare Your greatness."*

A Major Glitch

"Know that the Lord, He is God; it is He who has made us, and not we ourselves;
we are His people and the sheep of His pasture."
—Psalm 100:3

You might know the story of what happened to our royal parents. Sometime after they had been created to fulfill an incredible destiny, there was a big problem. It's described in Genesis 3.

➡ **Read and visualize the events of human history provided in Genesis 3.** Before you open your Bible, ask God to be with you as you read. Ask Him to give you wisdom and understanding.

It was a tiny test—just one tree in a gorgeous garden of plenty. Adam and Eve chose to give away their royal birthright (and ours), as well as their power to resist evil, when they said yes to Satan's temptation and ignored God. *"Man, originally created in God's image, lost the divine likeness by committing sin"* (*Manuscript Releases,* vol. 3, p. 434).

Janene and I have been to countries in which slavery is a common practice. While working in Bangladesh, we discovered to our dismay that a little girl we had befriended was going to be sold. The family needed the money and was going to sell their own precious child as a slave or to be used as a prostitute. We "bought" her instead—for the price of a medium pizza!—to prevent this tragic mistake. Sadly, it was too late for the human race.

Do you realize that by the actions of Adam and Eve, you also were sold into slavery?

☐ yes
☐ no

Perhaps you think God is really the one at fault. Do you hold any resentment against Him for your present situation or circumstances? Share your thoughts:

_____
_____
_____

The Lord has provided us with greater detail regarding our sad situation:

*"For we do not wrestle against flesh and blood, but against principalities, against powers,
against the rulers of the darkness of this age, against spiritual hosts
of wickedness in the heavenly places"* (Eph. 6:12).

*"Man was the crowning act of the creation . . . designed to be a counterpart of God;
but Satan has labored to obliterate the image of God in man,
and to imprint upon him his own image"* (*Review and Herald,* June 18, 1895).

*"Be sober, be vigilant; because your adversary the devil
walks about like a roaring lion, seeking whom he may devour"* (1 Peter 5:8).

What do you think about the following statement: "Since I was sold to the devil, I cannot resist him"? It is . . .

☐ true

☐ false

We cannot resist the devil on our own. But outside help has been offered that will enable us to resist him. **Enter God!** He purchased us back, but it cost Him far more than money!

> *"You were not redeemed with corruptible things, like silver or gold,*
> *from your aimless conduct . . . but with the precious blood of Christ,*
> *as of a lamb without blemish and without spot"* (1 Peter 1:18, 19).

> *"Man sold himself to Satan, but Jesus bought back the race, redeeming men and women*
> *from the slavery of a cruel tyrant"* (*Bible Echo*, Oct. 15, 1900).

On Day 3 you will study this subject in greater detail—but right now, what do you think of God buying you out of slavery?

_____

_____

_____

➡ **Taking time with the Lord.** Meditate on 1 Peter 1:18, 19, then share your thoughts with the One who bought you by paying with His life.

> *"Know that the Lord, He is God;*
> *it is He who has made us, and*
> *not we ourselves; we are His people*
> *and the sheep of His pasture."*

Amazing Rescue

"Eye has not seen, nor ear heard, nor have entered into the heart of man
the things which God has prepared for those who love Him."
—1 Corinthians 2:9

"Through the efficacy of Christ's sacrifice we may stand before God
pure and spotless, with our sins pardoned and atoned for."
—Ellen G. White*

Let's again turn to the harrowing account in Genesis 3. Describe what is happening in verses 8 and 9:

_____

_____

_____

The Lord could not stand being separated from His children! He just had to talk with Adam and Eve. He told them He would pay the wages of sin—death, which they earned through disobedience to God's law.

*"But with the precious blood of Christ, as of a lamb without blemish and without spot. He indeed was foreordained **before the foundation of the world,** but was manifest in these last times for you"* (1 Peter 1:19, 20).

The bold portion of this Bible passage is amazing! What do you think it means?

_____

_____

_____

"The salvation of the human race has ever been the object of the councils of heaven. The covenant of mercy was made before the foundation of the world. It has existed from all eternity" (Signs of the Times, June 12, 1901).

The Father, Son, and Holy Spirit knew from eternity that you would fall and inflict great suffering upon Them and yourself, but They love you so much They decided that, long before you were created, Jesus would suffer and die for you—so you could share "forever" with Them!

Do you realize just how much the Lord loves you and has done for you?

☐ I didn't realize God loved me as much as He does.

☐ I fully understand God's love for me.

☐ I want to understand more of His love and what it means to me.

Explain your answer more fully:

_____

The Godhead developed a plan whereby the Father and Son would experience a horrific separation at the cross. When Jesus took your sins upon Himself, it threatened to rip the pair apart forever! Read Matthew 27:26 and realize that this hideous moment in time happened to Jesus so you would never need to experience it.

On top of all this, Jesus would give up His omnipresence (power to be everywhere at one time) forever. Wow! Are you thankful for Their amazing love and grace? Share this moment with God and tell Him how thankful you are that He loves you so very much.

_____

_____

_____

God's greatest desire is to be with you. Let's follow this line of thought through the Bible. Fill in the blanks . . .

- Genesis 5:22: "Enoch _____ with God."
- Genesis 6:9: "Noah _____ with God."
- Exodus 25:8: "Let them make me a sanctuary, that I may _____ among them."
- Matthew 1:23: "Behold, the virgin shall _____, and bear a Son, and they shall call His name Immanuel, which is translated, '_____.'"
- John 1:14: "The Word became flesh and _____ among us."
- John 15:5: "I am the vine, you are the branches. He who _____ in Me, and _____, bears much fruit."
- John 14:16: "I will pray the Father, and He will give you another Helper, that He may _____ forever."

John 14:20 says, "At that day you will know that I am in My Father, and you in Me, and I in you." In the space provided below, diagram as best you can this statement from Jesus.

Grasp this heavenly concept and ponder its implications upon your life.

Scripture leaves no doubt—God wants to be with us! Would you like to experience God dwelling in you right now? Invite Him to come in! **Write your invitation to Him:**

_____

_____

_____

_____

_____

➡ **Taking time with the Lord.** Don't forget to thank Him in prayer that He has accepted and answered your invitation.

> *"Eye has not seen, nor ear heard, nor have entered into the heart of man the things which God has prepared for those who love Him."*

Review and Herald, Aug. 4, 1896.

Daily Display

God uses the word "good" seven times during the Creation account found in Genesis, chapter 1. "God saw everything that He had made, and indeed it was very good. So the evening and the morning were the sixth day."
—Genesis 1:31

"A state of mind that sees God in everything
is evidence of growth in grace and a thankful heart."
—Charles G. Finney

It's been said that nature is God's "second book." As flowers reflect sunlight in each colorful petal, as birds sing their lovely, complex melodies, and as clouds dance across the sky, we are reminded of the God who reveals His love for us even in a sin-laden world. His handiwork is designed to bring us continual moments of pleasure as we walk with Him.

At one point in my Christian experience, I read the following quote and was disturbed—I just didn't have the degree of joy in my life that the redeemed were exhibiting: *A glorious light shone all about their heads, and they were continually shouting and offering praises to God* (*The Adventist Home*, p. 546).

Don't panic if you're not there either! The good news is that this is a growing experience. As you spend time with the Lord, your relationship and walk matures. Today I find myself thanking God for even the tiny things. But I had to work to get there, which I did by guarding my time with God and learning to walk with Him more closely.

Your Assignment for Day 4

Take some time today to go on a walk in nature somewhere, weather permitting. As you walk, be very aware that Jesus is walking with you. Share your thoughts and feelings with Him; if no one else is around, you might want to talk aloud with Him. If you are in a city, it can be challenging to discover nature; but even as I write, I'm looking out of a city window and can see the leaves of maple trees glowing bright green because they have recently been dowsed by rain and are now brightly reflecting rays of sunlight. What a joyful reminder that soon we will dwell in a land that has no need of the sun because God is our light!

On Your Walk . . .

"As you behold these works of nature's let your mind be carried up higher to nature's God; let it be elevated to the Creator of the universe, and then adore the Creator who has made all these beautiful things for your benefit, for your happiness" (*Review and Herald*, May 31, 1870).

"In His teaching from nature, Christ was speaking of the things which His own hands had made, and which had qualities and powers that He Himself had imparted. . . . To Adam and Eve in their Eden home nature was full of the knowledge of God, teeming with divine instruction. Wisdom spoke to the eye and was received into the heart" (*Christ's Object Lessons*, p. 18).

After Your Walk . . .

Write down some of your thoughts and feelings experienced during your time with God. Here are some ideas to guide your thoughts and spark some ideas (check those that apply and expand upon them below):

- ☐ What happened on your walk that was pleasant? Or was it an unpleasant time? Why?
- ☐ Did you sense God's presence with you? Did you like it?
- ☐ Was this time of communion with God different than your time with Him in the past?
- ☐ Was this an experience that you would like to repeat?
- ☐ Did you find yourself praising God on your walk?

_____

_____

_____

_____

_____

Further Contemplation:

"Jesus plucked the beautiful lily, and placed it in the hands of children and youth; and as they looked into His own youthful face, fresh with the sunlight of His Father's countenance, He gave the lesson, 'Consider the lilies of the field, how they grow; . . . they toil not, neither do they spin; and yet I say unto you, that even Solomon in all his glory was not arrayed like one of these.' Then followed the sweet assurance and the important lesson, 'Wherefore, if God so clothe the grass of the field, which today is, and tomorrow is cast into the oven, shall He not much more clothe you, O ye of little faith?'

"In the sermon on the mount these words were spoken to others besides children and youth. They were spoken to the multitude, among whom were men and women full of worries and perplexities, and sore with disappointment and sorrow. Jesus continued: 'Therefore take no thought, saying, What shall we eat? or, What shall we drink? or, Wherewithal shall we be clothed? (for after all these things do the Gentiles seek:) for your Heavenly Father knoweth that ye have need of all these things.' Then spreading out His hands to the surrounding multitude, He said, 'But seek ye first the kingdom of God, and His righteousness; and all these things shall be added unto you'" (Christ's Object Lessons, p. 19).

Is there anything you gleaned from today's walk in nature that God is leading you to do or to understand? If so, what is it?

_____

_____

_____

➡ **Taking time with the Lord.** Let the Lord know in prayer how you choose to respond to His leading in your life.

> **God uses the word "good" seven times during the Creation account found in Genesis 1.**
>
> "God saw everything that He had made, and indeed it was very good. So the evening and the morning were the sixth day."

Look a Little Higher

"Lift up your eyes on high, and see who has created these things, who brings out their host by number; He calls them all by name, by the greatness of His might and the strength of His power; not one is missing."
—Isaiah 40:26

"The early Christians were looking not for a cleft in the ground called a grave, but for a cleavage in the sky called Glory."
—Alexander MacLaren

Let's visit heaven. Begin today by taking time to read the following texts:

- Revelation 21:1-7
- Revelation 22:1-6

Share at least two important things God is telling you in these verses:

_____

_____

Here are two truths that continue to amaze me:

- God is moving His government to earth; it will become the center of the universe!
- God will spend eternity with us on the earth made new!

A Vision of the New Earth

"With Jesus at our head we all descended from the City down to this earth, on a great and mighty mountain, which could not bear Jesus up, and it parted asunder, and there was a mighty plain. Then we looked up and saw the Great City, with twelve foundations, twelve gates . . . and an angel at each gate. We all cried out 'The City, the Great City, it's coming, it's coming down from God out of heaven;' and it came and settled on the place where we stood. Then we began to look at the glorious things outside of the City. There I saw most glorious houses, that had the appearance of silver, supported by four pillars, set with pearls, most glorious to behold, which were to be inhabited by the saints, and in them was a golden shelf. I saw many of the saints go into the houses, take off their glittering crowns and lay them on the shelf, then go out into the field by the houses to do something with the earth; not as we have to do with the earth here; no, no. A glorious light shone all about their heads and they were continually shouting and offering praises to God" (Review and Herald, July 21, 1851).

"Then an angel bore me gently down to this dark world [earth]. Sometimes I think I can stay here no longer; all things of earth look so dreary. I feel very lonely here, for I have seen a better land" (Early Writings, p. 20).

Have you seen the better world that God has prepared for those who love Him? In your studies, have you tasted the paradise to come?

Share your thoughts: _____

_____

_____

"All the treasures of the universe will be open to the study of God's redeemed. . . . And the years of eternity, as they roll, will bring richer and still more glorious revelations of God and of Christ. As knowledge is progressive, so will love, reverence, and happiness increase. The more men learn of God, the greater will be their admiration of His character" (*The Adventist Home,* p. 548).

> *"The Spirit and the bride say, 'Come!' And let him who hears say, 'Come!' . . .*
> *Whoever desires, let him take the water of life freely"* (Rev. 22:17).

➡ **Read John 14:1-3**

Do you believe one of these mansions has your name on its door?

☐ no

☐ yes

☐ not sure

What are your thoughts at this moment?

_____

_____

_____

➡ **Now read John 14:4-7.**

Thomas had a problem, but what did Jesus tell him? Do you have the same problem as Thomas? How did Jesus' answer strike you?

_____

_____

_____

Jesus told Thomas that it was all about a relationship! "I am the way," He said. You see, if you know Jesus, you have already received the occupancy agreement signed in His blood. You are only waiting for the delivery date to take effect!

It Gets Even Better

Revelation 3:21 says, "To him who overcomes I will grant to sit with Me on My throne, as I also overcame and sat down with My Father on His throne."

Not only is the center of the universe going to be relocated so God can be with us forever, He is going to move one step closer in abiding with us by inviting us to join Him on His throne. Ask God to help you grasp the vision of this future and the blessings to come, which are prepared for all those who love God with all of their hearts.

Would you like to thank God for all He has done for you? You see, in the mind of God, He has already seated you on His throne and moved you into your mansion.

➡ **It's now your choice!**

☐ I choose to be in heaven with the Lord and believe in His promises.

☐ I want to believe—but I need help!

➡ **Taking time with the Lord.** Pray the following: "Father, I do believe, but please help my unbelief. I want a better relationship with the Way—Jesus. Help me to focus upon You, Your soon coming, and the better world You have prepared for me. I don't have the strength to look away from this present world, but I choose to look at You. Please give me the power to make it a reality! Thank You for Your love and for answering my prayer. In Jesus' name, amen."

> *"Lift up your eyes on high, and see who has created these things, who brings out their host by number; He calls them all by name, by the greatness of His might and the strength of His power; not one is missing."*

2

Born Again

"The second birth is scarcely less perplexing to the theologian
than the first to the embryologist."
—Henry Drummond

After the disaster in Eden, the human race tested 100 percent positive for the "sin gene." And if we are going to make it to eternity, our sin-polluted gene pool must experience a drastic alteration. We need a DNA transfusion of major proportions. Enter God Himself, implanted in the virgin Mary—bioengineering of the heavenly kind! Fallen humanity was again brought near to God. And now, because the human gene pool was infused with divine genes, we have the opportunity to choose which genes are to flourish in our human temples.

The Dalai Lama once said, "I am a man of religion, but religion alone cannot answer all our problems." While he was thinking along different lines, I am going to use his quote to illustrate a biblical truth. You might be a religious person attending church on a regular basis but still be lost.

That was Nicodemus' problem. He was a respected religious leader, but he needed more than a framework of religion. The key to salvation is found in forming a lifelong friendship with the Lord. Once you are reborn into the family of God and daily choose to follow your new Master, the DNA transfer continues, resulting in the eventual eradication of the sin gene.

"When the Spirit of God controls mind and heart, the converted soul breaks forth into a new song; for he realizes that in his experience the promise of God has been fulfilled, that his transgression has been forgiven, his sin covered. . . . But because this experience is his, the Christian is not therefore to fold his hands, content with that which has been accomplished for him. He who has determined to enter the spiritual kingdom will find that all the powers and passions of unregenerate nature, backed by the forces of the kingdom of darkness, are arrayed against him. Each day he must renew his consecration, each day do battle with evil. Old habits, hereditary tendencies to wrong, will strive for the mastery, and against these he is to be ever on guard, striving in Christ's strength for victory" (The Acts of the Apostles, pp. 476, 477).

Shaping Jesus Into My Image

"The Lord is not slack concerning His promise, as some count slackness,
but is longsuffering toward us, not willing that any should perish
but that all should come to repentance."
—2 Peter 3:9

What do you think this chapter title means in relationship to Christianity today and to you in particular?

_____

_____

_____

*"His disciples . . . said, 'Lord, do You want us to command fire to come down
from heaven and consume them, just as Elijah did?' But He turned and rebuked them,
and said, 'You do not know what manner of spirit you are of. For the Son of Man
did not come to destroy men's lives but to save them'"* (Luke 9:54-56).

The disciples were convinced that they would be doing God's will in destroying the village. They were walking with Him but completely missed the true character of Christ!

I must evaluate my walk with God based upon (choose all that apply):

☐ my thoughts
☐ the way I feel
☐ the sure word of Scripture
☐ how successful I am
☐ listening to the Good Shepherd

You cannot base your Christian experience on your thoughts or feelings—you must be guided by the Holy Spirit through the Word of God.

"We are starting to redefine Christianity. We are giving in to the dangerous temptation to take the Jesus of the Bible and twist him into a version of Jesus we are more comfortable with.

"A nice, middle-class, American Jesus. A Jesus who doesn't mind materialism and who would never call us to give away everything we have. A Jesus who would not expect us to forsake our closest relationships so that he receives all our affection. A Jesus who is fine with nominal devotion that does not infringe on our comforts, because, after all, he loves us just the way we are. A Jesus who wants us to be balanced, who . . . wants us to avoid dangerouse extremes. . . . A Jesus who brings us comfort and prosperity as we live out our Christian spin on the American dream.

"But do you and I realize what we are doing at this point? We are molding Jesus into our image. He is beginning to look a lot like us because, after all, that is whom we are most comfortable with. And the danger now is that when we gather in our church buildings to sing and lift up our hands in worship, we may not actually be worshiping the Jesus of the Bible. Instead we may be worshiping ourselves" (David Platt, *Radical* [New York: Multnomah, 2010], p. 13).

It's time for a personal checkup. **Pray and then ask yourself, "Have I been shaping Jesus into my image?**

☐ yes

☐ no

☐ not sure

If you answered yes or not sure, identify the things in your life that are a problem:

_____ _____

_____ _____

_____ _____

Do you have problem areas? You might wonder, "What now? Is there hope?" Yes! You can know with certainty that God is willing and able to help you to change . . . if you are willing.

> *"The will must be placed on the side of God's will. You are not able, of yourself, to bring your purposes and desires and inclinations into submission to the will of God; but if you are 'willing to be made willing,' God will accomplish the work for you, even 'casting down imaginations, and every high thing that exalteth itself against the knowledge of God, and bringing into captivity every thought to the obedience of Christ'"* (*Signs of the Times*, May 18, 1904).

If you are ready now, ask the Lord to make you willing to be made willing. He will answer your prayer. And soon, you will not miss those things that once tied you to this world. You can break free! Continue to make this same request each day and it won't be long before the joy in your life will be overflowing.

➡ **Taking time with the Lord.** If you are not yet willing to ask God to change you, tell Him why in prayer. He will be glad to listen!

> *"The Lord is not slack concerning His promise,*
> *as some count slackness,*
> *but is longsuffering toward us, not willing*
> *that any should perish*
> *but that all should come to repentance."*

When You Are Converted

"The law of the Lord is perfect, converting the soul;
the testimony of the Lord is sure, making wise the simple."
—Psalm 19:7

Read the following texts:
- Matthew 18:3
- Luke 22:31-34

Can you walk alongside God and not be converted? Explain your answer below.

_____

_____

_____

Peter spent a great deal of time with Jesus and was still unconverted. Describe your walk with Christ (check all that apply):

- ☐ I am walking a little behind the Master.
- ☐ I am so close to Him that the dust of His sandals is falling on me.
- ☐ I don't listen to Him all of the time.
- ☐ I listen to Him all of the time.
- ☐ I want to walk closer to Him and listen better.
- ☐ I'm not even on the same pathway.
- ☐ other: _____.

➡ **Read Acts 28:26, 27.**

What do you sense God is saying to you at this moment?

_____

_____

_____

Did you notice that the heart of the people had "grown dull"? In other words, they felt they had everything and that they didn't need what God was offering. They had closed their eyes and stopped their ears to the Word of God.

Likewise, the disciples were so polluted with the teachings and customs of their day that they had a difficult time understanding what Christ was trying to teach them. He yearned to share more, but it was too much for them to accept (John 16:12). Instead, much of their time was spent arguing about who was going to be the greatest in the kingdom.

The Greek word for "converted" in the New Testament is in the active voice, meaning it is something that you must do—to turn. Think of walking down a path and, as you do, you make the decision to turn around and travel in the opposite direction; this is the meaning of Christ's counsel to be converted. It is not something done for you. You must be an active participant! Dietrich Bonhoeffer stated it perfectly: "When Christ calls a man, he bids him come and die."

Have you chosen to turn—to be active—to die to self today and allow God to take full control of your life?

☐   yes

☐   no

☐   most of the time

☐   some of the time

What do you think "dying to self" really means?

_____

_____

_____

How do you think God feels about your answer at this moment?

_____

_____

_____

Are there things holding you back from complete surrender right now? If so, list them here:

1. _____

2. _____

3. _____

4. _____

> *"Jesus called a little child to Him, set him in the midst of them, and said,*
> *'Assuredly, I say to you, unless you are converted and become as little children,*
> *you will by no means enter the kingdom of heaven'"* (Matt. 18:2, 3).

➡ **Read Matthew 18:1.**

Notice that Jesus did not answer the question of who would be the greatest in the kingdom; rather, He addressed the real question: Would they end up in the kingdom at all? Christ's tone is severe. This is serious stuff, and the Lord wants to make certain that everyone understands what the requirements are for entering heaven.

➡ **Read Luke 22:31, 32.**

Describe the significance of this passage as it applies to your life:

_____

_____

_____

Did you notice that Jesus was concerned for Peter and prayed for him? Well, He is just as concerned for you! He tells us that the Holy Spirit even presents your prayers in the very best light to the Father. So even though you might not be very good at praying or might not know exactly what to pray about, the Holy Spirit will package all of your troubles, trials, and bumbles and stumbles, presenting them to the Father in perfect and absolute beauty.

➡ **Taking time with the Lord.** Pray the following: "Father, I need You so much. I want to be converted, and I choose to die to self today and every day. Make me willing to be made willing. Take all of me. I give myself to You right now just as I am. Help me to become like You. Thank You for loving me, dying for me, and caring for me." Don't stop praying—keep communicating your feelings to Him in your own words.

I Will Follow You

"Your ears shall hear a word behind you, saying, 'This is the way, walk in it,'
whenever you turn to the right hand or whenever you turn to the left."
—Isaiah 30:21

"Lord, send me anywhere, only go with me. Lay any burden on me, only sustain me.
Sever any ties but the tie that binds me to Thy service and to Thy heart."
—David Livingstone

The devil hungered to have Peter as his own, but Christ prayed for His disciple—and His prayer was fulfilled in an interesting way. Peter was truly converted during a tragic moment when his heart was broken. You remember the story. As all the vile rage and cursing spewed from his lips, the young fisherman turned and saw Jesus in the judgment hall staring directly into his eyes. There was no condemnation in Christ's face, only sadness. His gaze ripped into Peter's heart. Blinded by a flood of tears, Peter stumbled back to the Garden of Gethsemane, the sad eyes of Jesus burned into his mind—he wished he could die!

That was Peter's moment of turning. That was the instant he died. From that day forward he never trusted himself again. Peter was eventually nailed to a cross for his unwavering faith, but he asked to be crucified upside down because he felt unworthy to die in the same manner as his Lord.

John and his brother were once labeled as "sons of thunder," but eventually they surrendered their lives completely to God's leading. Scripture speaks of John as "the one Jesus loved," and tradition says that he was boiled in oil but was unharmed. He was later banished to the rocky isle of Patmos to live in exile. No tribulation was too great to suffer for his Lord.

The apostle Paul was a religious man in the extreme. He ate, drank, and slept religion—but he was a killer who thought he was doing God's will. With papers in hand, signed by the religious leaders in Jerusalem, he was on a mission to Damascus to slaughter more Christians when he encountered God!

> "He said, 'Who are You, Lord?' Then the Lord said, 'I am Jesus, whom you are persecuting.
> It is hard for you to kick against the goads.'" Now notice Paul's response:
> "So he, trembling and astonished, said, 'Lord, what do You want me to do?'" (Acts 9:5, 6).

When Paul looked into the face of Christ, his conversion was immediate. He experienced the "turning" in his life, and he was ready to follow his God—regardless of the cost.

➡ **Read 2 Corinthians 11:23-33**

Consider what Paul went through. What is the reason each man endured what he did?

_____

_____

_____

➡ **Read the following verses; circle each place where the word "love"/"loves"/"loved" is found.**

"I have set before you life and death, blessing and cursing; therefore choose life,
that both you and your descendants may live; that you may love the Lord your God,
that you may obey His voice, and that you may cling to Him, for He is your life and the length of your days;
and that you may dwell in the land which the Lord swore to your fathers" (Deut. 30:19, 20).

"He who has My commandments and keeps them, it is he who loves Me.
And he who loves Me will be loved by My Father, and I will love him and manifest Myself to him" (John 14:21).

"Who shall separate us from the love of Christ? Shall tribulation, or distress, or persecution,
or famine, or nakedness, or peril, or sword? . . . Yet in all these things we are more than conquerors
through Him who loved us. For I am persuaded that neither death nor life,
nor angels nor principalities nor powers, nor things present nor things to come, nor height nor depth,
nor any other created thing, shall be able to separate us from the love of God
which is in Christ Jesus our Lord" (Rom. 8:35, 37-39).

"In this the love of God was manifested toward us, that God has sent His only begotten Son
into the world, that we might live through Him. . . . And we have known and believed
the love that God has for us. God is love, and he who abides in love abides in God,
and God in him. Love has been perfected among us in this: that we may have boldness
in the day of judgment; because as He is, so are we in this world. There is no fear in love;
but perfect love casts out fear, because fear involves torment. But he who fears has not been made perfect in love.
We love Him because He first loved us" (1 John 4:9-19).

Every disciple of Christ will decide to follow Him at any cost to self, because they have fallen in love with Him. The love relationship becomes so powerful, so pervasive, that people are willing to do *all* for their Best Friend.

When he was a teenager, Hudson Taylor accepted Christ and experienced God's call to serve in China. On September 19, 1853, Taylor left England for China—a voyage by sea that would take almost six months. The following is his own account of leaving his home and mother behind for God:

"She sat by my side, and joined me in the last hymn that we should sing together before the long parting. We knelt down, and she prayed—the last mother's prayer I was to hear before starting for China.

"Then notice was given that we must separate, and we had to say goodbye, never expecting to meet on earth again. For my sake she restrained her feelings as much as possible. We parted; and she went on shore, giving me her blessing! I stood alone on deck, and she followed the ship as we moved towards the dock gates. As we passed through the gates, and the separation really commenced, I shall never forget the cry of anguish wrung from that mother's heart. It went through me like a knife. I never knew so fully, until then, what God so loved the world meant. And I am quite sure that my precious mother learned more of the love of God to the perishing in that hour than in all her life before."

As you consider the lives given to Christ in our study today, are you ready to do the same—to make any commitment, any sacrifice, and to go anywhere God may call you?

☐ yes

☐ no

☐ maybe

Explain your answer: _____

Are there adjustments that need to be made in an area of your life so you can fully follow the Lord as He desires that you should?

- ☐ in my thinking (my potential, my mind-set about life, my attitude)
- ☐ in my relationships (my family, friends, business associates, others)
- ☐ in my employment (is it an anchor to my experience, my spirituality?)
- ☐ in my actions or nonaction (how I pray and study, spend my time)
- ☐ other: _____.

➥ **Taking time with the Lord.** Do you sense God leading you to follow Him closer today than ever before—to make adjustments in your life? Pray and ask Him for help now.

> *"Your ears shall hear a word behind you, saying,*
> *'This is the way, walk in it,' whenever you turn to the right*
> *hand or whenever you turn to the left."*

Gold and Silver Have I None

"Create in me a clean heart, O God, and renew a steadfast spirit within me."
—Psalm 51:10

In my travels for the TV series *Making Waves*, I have the opportunity to share amazing stories from around the world demonstrating God's wonder-working power in people's lives. The following is one such story:

Ragasa, the Witch

Ragasa has large eyes that radiate love, but that was not always the case. As a little girl, she grew up with demons in her home. They were not only seen by all of her family—they also carried on regular conversations with them as well.

When she was a little older, the demons said to her, "We would like you to become a witch, and if you agree, we will give you great power." She agreed.

They then instructed her, "Go down to the river." As commanded, Ragasa made her way to the water's edge. There the demons told her to go "down into the water." She did as they said, and, according to her, she spent the next day and a half under water.

At this moment I stopped the interview because I thought the interpreter had made a mistake. I asked her to repeat what she had said. And as it turned out, I had heard it right—she had lived under water for more than a day. "While there," she explained, "the demons fed me and took care of me." This was all under water—but it doesn't end there! "They then gave me great powers, such as control over lightning. I could be shot with a gun and not be hurt. One day an army came to take over my village, but I created potions that kept them away."

The devil has great power. If you think you can contest against this much power, you are greatly mistaken. The Gospels are replete with stories of Satan's power. The apostle Paul wrote that we are not fighting "against flesh and blood, but against principalities, against powers, against the rulers of the darkness of this age, against spiritual hosts of wickedness in the heavenly places" (Eph. 6:12).

But we have a mighty Champion who fights for us. And when He lives in you, the devil cannot defeat you. Ragasa's testimony bears witness to this truth!

"One day the demons were mad at me, and they made me very sick. I went to doctors, but they could do nothing for me. I spent much time in bed." She had learned what most of us know all too well: The devil is sly. At first sin fascinates; then it assassinates.

"A little later two young women came to me and said, 'There is a God in heaven who can heal you. Can we pray for you?' I thought, *Well, the devil hasn't been doing anything for me lately, so go ahead.* So they prayed for me, and I was immediately healed. Then they told me to learn about Jesus, that it would be a blessing to me. I did as they said, and I fell in love with Jesus and was soon baptized in the river next to my home."

But even at her baptism, the devil was desperate to steal her away from God. "As I came up out of the water, the devil burned my house to the ground. I poked through the ashes after they cooled, looking for my Bible. When I found it, I saw that it hadn't been touched by the fire or the smoke. Because of that miracle, many people in my village believed in God."

When speaking in the United States, people often ask me, "Why don't we see those kinds of miracles happen here?" **Why do you think?**

_____

_____

_____

➡ **Read Acts 3:1-8 to help find an answer.**

Imagine Peter standing before this beggar who had never walked a day in his life; the poor fellow was hoping for scraps of money in the pockets of passersby. He became excited when he saw Peter pull out his left cloak pocket—but it was empty! No money, just lint. The man was probably wondering what was going on, but then Peter spoke, "Silver and gold I do not have, but what I do have I give you: In the name of Jesus Christ of Nazareth, rise up and walk!" Immediately, the man who had never felt a pebble pushed into the sole of his foot stood up and rejoiced in God.

What is it that Peter had?

_____

_____

_____

Peter had the Holy Spirit because He was a converted daily follower of Christ. He had turned around and now the God of heaven was living inside of him, enabling him to do whatever God wanted him to do. "*As the will of man cooperates with the will of God, it becomes omnipotent*" (*Christ's Object Lessons,* p. 333).

Check the statements that apply to you:

☐ I can do everything God wants me to do if He is living in me.

☐ I am too weak to do anything.

☐ God is all-powerful.

☐ If God is living in me, I have the way, the truth, and the life in me.

☐ In order to have all of God, I must surrender to Him.

☐ I still need some silver and gold to survive in this world.

☐ I'm not sure how it all works.

☐ other: _____.

Dwight L. Moody said, "Our greatest fear should not be of failure, but of succeeding at something that doesn't really matter."

List those things that shouldn't matter in your life:

- _____

- _____

- _____

- _____

Especially in America, we have much wealth but little of the Holy Spirit. It can be a real challenge to focus on Jesus and choose Him.

- If you could have all the gold in the world *or* Jesus, which would you choose? _____
- If you could have fame *or* Jesus, which would you choose? _____
- If you could have all the powers of Ragasa *or* have Jesus, which would you choose? _____
- If you could have it all for 70 years *or* eternity with Jesus, which do you choose? _____

➡ **Taking time with the Lord.** Someone once said, "To get something you never had, you have to do something you never did." Talk with Jesus about your life's direction, your goals, your commitment. Perhaps you don't want to talk right now, but take a moment to tell Him why you don't want to talk. If you're comfortable, write out your thoughts:

_____

_____

_____

_____

{ *"Create in me a clean heart, O God, and renew a steadfast spirit within me."* }

The Cost of Commitment

"Be anxious for nothing, but in everything by prayer and supplication,
with thanksgiving, let your requests be made known to God;
and the peace of God, which surpasses all understanding,
will guard your hearts and minds through Christ Jesus."
—Philippians 4:6, 7

"Wherever you are, be all there."
—Jim Elliot, missionary martyr

Jesus said, "You shall love the Lord your God with all your heart, with all your soul, with all your mind, and with all your strength" (Mark 12:30).

How does, or should, this statement from Jesus impact your life?

_____

_____

Woody Allen once said that one way to make God laugh is to tell Him your future plans. God is seeking those who will commit all of their plans to Him and trust fully in His leading. What does this commitment look like? What does it cost? While in Africa, David Livingstone provided this down-to-earth statement of commitment:

"If you have men who will only come if they know there is a good road,
I don't want them. I want men who will come if there is no road at all."

In our era of megachurches and "feel-good" worship services, we discover an interesting contrast in commitment as to how the Bible describes it. Look at how Jesus interacted with those who came seeking Him, as recorded in Luke 9:57-62:

"Someone said to Him, 'Lord, I will follow You wherever You go.' And Jesus said to him, 'Foxes have holes and birds of the air have nests, but the Son of Man has nowhere to lay His head.' Then He said to another, 'Follow Me.' But he said, 'Lord, let me first go and bury my father.' Jesus said to him, 'Let the dead bury their own dead, but you go and preach the kingdom of God.' And another also said, 'Lord, I will follow You, but let me first go and bid them farewell who are at my house.' But Jesus said to him, 'No one, having put his hand to the plow, and looking back, is fit for the kingdom of God.'"

If Jesus talked to you like this, how would you respond to Him?

_____

_____

Based upon today's churches and their constant message to meet the "felt needs" of the seeker, Jesus really missed the mark! Today many are ready to bring anyone into the fold regardless of their commitment to Christ—just to grow the membership! But Jesus wasn't finished on this topic; He had more to say:

"When Jesus heard these things, He said to him, 'You still lack one thing.
Sell all that you have and distribute to the poor, and you will have
treasure in heaven; and come, follow Me.' But when he heard this,
he became very sorrowful, for he was very rich" (Luke 18:22, 23).

The disciples couldn't believe what Jesus told the young rich man. Didn't He realize the amount of money and influence this fellow possessed? Just imagine how he could have helped grow their church! **Would you have agreed with the disciples or with Jesus?**

☐ I agree with the disciples.

☐ I agree with Jesus.

☐ I'm not sure.

Christ described what total commitment to Him involved:

"Most assuredly, I say to you, unless you eat the flesh of the Son of Man and drink His blood,
you have no life in you. . . . For My flesh is food indeed, and My blood is drink indeed.
He who eats My flesh and drinks My blood abides in Me, and I in him. As the living Father sent Me,
and I live because of the Father, so he who feeds on Me will live because of Me" (John 6:53, 55-57).

Those around Jesus were absolutely shocked and disturbed. John 6:66 records their reaction: *"From that time many of His disciples went back and walked with Him no more."*

What is your reaction realizing that He is calling you to the same commitment?

_____

_____

_____

Don't be surprised that complete commitment to Christ is radical in the eyes of the world and to most church members. Real commitment to Christ costs all we are and all we possess. Many who listened to Him that day had "walked" with Jesus for some time but stopped because the journey of surrender cost more than they were willing to pay. They had attempted to shape Jesus into their own image, but that day the Light revealed the darkness of the human heart and, rather than rejoice in the Light, they turned away.

David Livingstone spent most of his life faithfully serving God in Africa. "I will place no value on anything I have or may possess except in relation to the kingdom of Christ." God might or might not be calling you to Africa, but He is calling you to place your complete trust in Him before all else!

➡ **Consider the following texts.** Take time to ponder each one and don't forget to pray first—asking God to anoint your eyes with spiritual insight.

1. Matthew 4:18-22

2. Matthew 9:9

3. John 1:43

What kind of commitment did these followers have? If you were to rate their commitment as a percentage, what would it be in each case?

_____

_____

"The work of the Spirit of God in a man is not a work that unfits him for the common duties of ordinary life. There is not to be one religion for business and another religion for the church. The work of the Spirit of God embraces the whole man, soul, body, and spirit. If the Word of God is cherished as an abiding principle in the heart, and held fast under all and every circumstance, man is brought, with his entrusted capabilities, under [subjection] to the Lord Jesus Christ. His undivided powers, even his thoughts, are brought into captivity to Christ. This is true sanctification. All the parts of the experience blend in complete harmony. He is 'wanting in nothing.' He does not keep part to himself, to do with just as he pleases" (*In Heavenly Places*, p. 190).

Your response to Jesus:

☐ I will follow You at any cost!

☐ Lord, I am scared—please help me.

☐ I am not sure, but I am willing to learn from You and grow.

☐ I am hesitant and unsure. Can You please help me?

➡ **Taking time with the Lord.** Continue your walk with Him today. Share your innermost thoughts, feelings, and desires with Him in prayer.

"Be anxious for nothing, but in everything by prayer and supplication, with thanksgiving, let your requests be made known to God; and the peace of God, which surpasses all understanding, will guard your hearts and minds through Christ Jesus."

The God of Second Chances

The Bible has many examples of them—David, Samson, Peter, and more. Plus, there are countless examples outside of the Bible . . . such as yours truly! I'm talking about those who were given a second chance to board the bus bound for eternity.

Each of these people turned from God at some point in their lives, spurned His love, and, in so doing, caused Him and themselves tremendous pain. But God never gives up on anyone! Remember reading about Peter's conversion experience in the last unit? After looking into the eyes of Christ, he was devastated and felt as though he was lost forever—but Jesus commissioned two angels to give Peter a message.

After Christ's resurrection, two celestial beings waited at the tomb until the women came to embalm the body of their Lord. The story is found in Mark 16. After the shock of the discovery had worn off for the women, an incredible message was given to them. *"Go, tell His disciples—and Peter—that He is going before you into Galilee; there you will see Him, as He said to you"* (verse 7).

God is simply amazing! What a message for His heartbroken disciple: *"Peter, I still love you—and I want you to come home."*

The Bible is literally full of stories that unpack God's amazing desire for us to return to Him. *Regardless* of our previous actions against Him, He is ready to shower manifold blessings upon us. He is truly the God of second chances . . . and more!

Don't Go Too Far

"In every work that he began in the service of the house of God, in the law and in the
commandment, to seek his God, he did it with all his heart. So he prospered."
—2 Chronicles 31:21

When God was in the process of delivering the children of Israel from Egypt—a land that was also a symbol of sin and bondage—Pharaoh made a revealing statement: "I will let you go, that you may sacrifice to the Lord your God in the wilderness; only you shall not go very far away" (Ex. 8:28).

This is my take on the symbolism of the verse for our time: *It's OK to be a Christian if you wish and even do a few things for God—just don't go overboard and get too carried away with religion.*

One afternoon a friend came to my office and asked me how I arrived at the point of writing a book and study guide about Christian transformation. I shared with him that it represented a journey that encompassed many years of experiences—a journey that, by God's grace, will continue till Jesus comes. But it started at a very definite point in time!

After I played church for years, God gave me a clear second chance. While I was listening to a preacher speak, a divinely inspired flash of conviction hit me, and I realized that I was going to be eternally lost unless there were some drastic changes in my mode of thinking, my lifestyle, and my responses to God's powerful overtures to become my best friend.

My choices were clear-cut: Do I stay where I am—or do I go with God? (You can't do both!) Do I continue placing all of my energy into amassing money, houses, toys, and success, or do I begin to place God on the top of my priority list?

That very day I decided that God must play a more important role in my life. At the very least, I figured, He should move up the ladder a few rungs. That meager choice on my part was the beginning of my transformation process. Yes, it is a process!

How about you? How would you evaluate your present commitment to God? **Rate your level** on the continuum below using the following criteria: 1 equals "I have no desire to follow His will for my life," and 10 equals "I will do His will even if it costs me my life." Pray, search your heart, and then circle your answer:

1   2   3   4   5   6   7   8   9   10

Explain why you responded the way you did . . . and be honest with yourself.

_____

_____

_____

I'm assuming that you didn't circle 10, but if you did, that's wonderful; it would be my hope that you can still glean many things from this workbook that will enable you to climb higher in your relationship with Christ.

If you circled a lesser number, that's OK too! God is ready to work and walk with you forever at whatever point in the journey you're now walking.

Do you believe that God is ready to work and walk with you forever?

☐   Yes.

☐   No.

☐   I'm not sure what that really means.

Explain your answer:

_____

_____

The devil, like Pharaoh, is thrilled when you don't go too far in your relationship with God. He wants you to stay where you are—whether you circled a 3, 5, or 7. So are you ready to go all the way with Him? Are you ready to know Him as your best friend? If not, what is holding you back? Be specific.

_____

_____

_____

➡ **Read the following text through slowly,** and then reread it and contemplate each thought.

> *"Trust in the Lord with all your heart, and lean not on your own understanding;*
> *in all your ways acknowledge Him, and He shall direct your paths.*
> *Do not be wise in your own eyes; fear the Lord and depart from evil"* (Prov. 3:5-7).

➡ **Taking time with the Lord.** Spend time in prayer seeking God's help, asking Him to make His Word come alive within you.

> *"And in every work that he began in the service of the house of God,*
> *in the law and in the commandment, to seek his God,*
> *he did it with all his heart. So he prospered."*

Playing Church

"He answered and said to them, 'Well did Isaiah prophesy of you hypocrites, as it is written: "This people honors Me with their lips, but their heart is far from Me."'"
—Mark 7:6

Many people are Christ's by profession but the devil's by practice.

Judas played church to the bitter end. Peter played church too—but he eventually made a different choice when the reality of God's wonderful love finally hit home.

Satan is also very happy to let us "play" church as long as we don't get too serious about it. In addition, he doesn't get worried when we always make plans to leave Egypt but never actually do so. As Christians we must choose to follow God one day at a time—every day!

Are you willing to do more than play church today?

☐ No, I don't think I'm ready.
☐ I have so many other things competing for my time; I'm not sure.
☐ Yes, I am willing if God enables me to do so.
☐ My job and family take all of my time.
☐ I enjoy my novels, computer, or TV more than my Bible.
☐ other:_____.

Just prior to the exodus from Egypt, God spoke to Moses, saying, "This month shall be your beginning of months; it shall be the first month of the year to you" (Ex. 12:2).

➡ **Ponder:** Life begins when you are freed from the slavery of sin! The only way to be free is to allow Christ to enter your heart and liberate you.

What kind of commitment does God ask of us in our liberation? Both the Old and New Testament specifically address this. In the following two verses, **circle each word or phrase that speaks to the intensity of the commitment you must have in order to enjoy eternal life with Jesus.**

"You shall love the Lord your God with all your heart, with all your soul, and with all your strength" (Deut. 6:5).

"Behold, a certain lawyer stood up and tested Him, saying, 'Teacher, what shall I do to inherit eternal life?' He said to him, 'What is written in the law? What is your reading of it?' So he answered and said, '"You shall love the Lord your God with all your heart, with all your soul, with all your strength, and with all your mind," and "your neighbor as yourself."' And He said to him, 'You have answered rightly; do this and you will live'" (Luke 10:25-28).

Now **circle the words of commitment** in this passage:

"He who truly loves and fears God, striving with a singleness of purpose to do His will, will place his body, his mind, his heart, his soul, his strength, under service to God. . . . You are each living your probationary time day by day, obtaining your experience as the days pass; but you can go over the ground only once. Then let every precious moment be employed as you will wish it had been when the judgment shall sit and the books shall be opened. Our Lord will judge us according to the opportunities that we have had" (*In Heavenly Places*, p. 190).

Do you now have a clearer understanding of the commitment required to enter eternal life?

☐ Yes.

☐ No.

☐ I never gave it much thought before.

A vibrant and powerful life in Christ is possible for you! Are you ready to accept Jesus' invitation? He is ready to enable you to do far more than just "play church"!

Are you ready to allow Him total access to your life? Write down your answer and any other thoughts you might have.

_____

_____

_____

➡ **Taking time with the Lord.** Pray to God and ask Him to help you rise above just playing church.

"He answered and said to them, 'Well did Isaiah prophesy of you hypocrites, as it is written: "This people honors Me with their lips, but their heart is far from Me."'"

Please Come Home

"And you return to the Lord your God and obey His voice,
according to all that I command you today, you and your children,
with all your heart and with all your soul."
—Deuteronomy 30:2

Even most non-Christians have heard the story of the guy who was thrown off a ship and swallowed by a whale. Well, it might not have been a whale, but it is a true story nonetheless.

Jonah was running away from the call of God. The Lord said, "Go this way." But Jonah said, "No, I'm going another way!" It took a while—or rather a whale—for him to finally see things God's way and head in the right direction.

King David was a man who had deeply loved God, but then he departed from the Lord by succumbing to the sins of adultery and murder. God was trying to speak to David and keep him from sinning, but the fallen king said, "No, I'm going another way!" It was some time before he heard God's voice and turned around to go in the right direction.

A few years after I became a Christian, God called me to full-time ministry. But when the opportunity actually came to pastor a new church in Truckee, California, I said, "No, I'm going another way!" It took me years to see things God's way and head in the right direction.

The problem is that this world is strewn with the wreckage of those who have gone down to Christless graves, saying to God, "No, I'm going another way." When God offers you salvation, you need to say, "Yes, Lord." The good news is that if you have done your own thing, you still have time to respond! *But* the time is coming when it will be too late.

Have you said to God, "I'm going another way"?

☐ Not in so many words, but maybe in my actions.
☐ Yes, I have.
☐ No, I am following all He has revealed to me.
☐ No, but I sense I could be following Him more closely.
☐ other: _____.

"None are so vile, none have fallen so low, as to be beyond the working of this power. In all who will submit themselves to the Holy Spirit a new principle of life is to be implanted; the lost image of God is to be restored in humanity" (*Christ's Object Lessons*, p. 96).

➡ **Spend some quiet time reading and contemplating Psalm 136.**

Now that you've read this psalm and prayed, is there something you sense God could be saying to you or asking of you?

_____

_____

_____

How will you respond to Him?

_____

_____

The *Good News Bible*'s translation of Ephesians 2:1-6 really hits home.

"In the past you were spiritually dead because of your disobedience and sins. At that time you followed the world's evil way; you obeyed the ruler of the spiritual powers in space, the spirit who now controls the people who disobey God. Actually all of us were like them and lived according to our natural desires, doing whatever suited the wishes of our own bodies and minds. In our natural condition we, like everyone else, were destined to suffer God's anger. But God's mercy is so abundant, and his love for us is so great, that while we were spiritually dead in our disobedience he brought us to life with Christ. It is by God's grace that you have been saved. In our union with Christ Jesus he raised us up with him to rule with him in the heavenly world."

I have shortened the following story from its original size so I can share it with you here. It brings a lump to my throat every time I share this real-life drama from Brazil:

"Maria's husband had died when Christina was an infant. The young mother, stubbornly refusing opportunities to remarry, got a job and set out to raise her young daughter. And now, 15 years later, the worst years were over. Though Maria's salary as a maid afforded few luxuries, it was reliable, and it did provide food and clothes.

"And now Christina was old enough to get a job to help out. . . . [But] she spoke often of going to the city. She dreamed of trading her dusty neighborhood for exciting avenues and city life. Just the thought of this horrified her mother. Maria was always quick to remind Christina of the harshness of the streets. 'People don't know you there. Jobs are scarce, and the life is cruel. And besides, if you went there, what would you do for a living?'

"Maria knew exactly what Christina would do, or would have to do, for a living. That's why her heart broke when she awoke one morning to find her daughter's bed empty. Maria knew immediately where her daughter had gone. She also knew immediately what she must do to find her. She quickly threw some clothes in a bag, gathered up all her money, and ran out of the house.

"On her way to the bus stop she entered a drugstore to get one last thing. Pictures. She sat in the photograph booth, closed the curtain, and spent all she could on pictures of herself. With her purse full of small black-and-white photos, she boarded the next bus to Rio de Janeiro.

"Maria knew Christina had no way of earning money. She also knew that her daughter was too stubborn to give up. When pride meets hunger, a human will do things that were before unthinkable. Knowing this, Maria began her search. Bars, hotels, nightclubs, any place with the reputation for streetwalkers or prostitutes. She went to them all. And at each place she left her picture—taped on a bathroom mirror, tacked to a hotel bulletin board, fastened to a corner phone booth. And on the back of each photo she wrote a note.

"It wasn't too long before both the money and the pictures ran out, and Maria had to go home. The weary mother wept as the bus began its long journey back to her small village.

"It was a few weeks later that young Christina descended the hotel stairs. Her young face was tired. Her brown eyes no longer danced with youth, but spoke of pain and fear. Her laughter was broken. . . .

"As she reached the bottom of the stairs, her eyes noticed a familiar face. She looked again, and there on the lobby mirror was a small picture of her mother. Christina's eyes burned and her throat tightened as she walked across the room and removed the small photo. Written on the back was this compelling invitation. 'Whatever you have done, whatever you have become, it doesn't matter. Please come home'" (Max Lucado, *No Wonder They Call Him the Savior*

[Nashville: Thomas Nelson, 1986, 2004]).

Please come! If you are already home, praise God . . . but if you are not or sense you might not be fully in the center of His will for your life, come to Him now, because it doesn't matter what you've done or what you have become! Open your heart now—God is ready to live in you and give you His daily victory and peace.

➡ **Taking time with the Lord.** Tell Him in prayer that you want to be made willing to be made willing to come home—and to accept you no matter what you have done, because you are ready to turn around and head in the right direction with His loving, endless storehouse of help.

> *"And you return to the Lord your God and obey His voice,*
> *according to all that I command you today,*
> *you and your children, with all your heart and with all your soul."*

Something Too Hard for God

"Our greatest desire is that you may be subjects of grace. You will never
be saved against your will. You must prize salvation, and submit to be
saved in the Lord's appointed way."
—Ellen G. White*

"Yours, O Lord, is the greatness, the power and the glory, the victory and the majesty;
for all that is in heaven and in earth is Yours; Yours is the kingdom, O Lord,
and You are exalted as head over all. Both riches and honor come from You, and You
reign over all. . . . In Your hand it is to make great and to give strength to all"
—1 Chronicles 29:11, 12

Imagine that kind of power! So now when I ask you to list anything that is impossible for God to do or accomplish, you might think I am confused—but consider it anyway and see if you can come up with something:

_____

Did you give up? Well, there is one thing God "cannot" do—He cannot save you if you will not allow Him to. You see, the devil *can't* make you do anything against your will, and God *won't!* That's why today's lesson is all about getting a correct understanding of the human will.

➡ **Read Matthew 9:9.**

God called him, and Matthew responded! Billy Sunday made this astute observation regarding the call to Matthew:

"How long did that conversion take? How long did it take him to accept Christ after he had made up his mind? And you tell me you can't make an instant decision to please God? The decision of Matthew proves that you can. While he was sitting at his desk he was not a disciple. The instant he arose he was. That move changed his attitude toward God. Then he ceased to do evil and commenced to do good. You can be converted just as quickly as Matthew was.

"Rising and following Christ switched Matthew from the broad to the narrow way. He must have counted the cost as he would have balanced his cash book. He put one side against the other. The life he was living led to all chance of gain. On the other side there was Jesus, and Jesus outweighs all else. He saw the balance turn as the tide of a battle turns and then it ended with his decision. The sinner died and the disciple was born."

Describe what happened to Matthew in your own words. How do you account for his actions?

_____

_____

➡ **Read and consider the following verses:**

- Matthew 16:24
- 1 Kings 18:21
- Joshua 24:15
- Isaiah 1:18-20

Identify the common thread that runs through these texts:

_____

_____

Our entire relationship with God is based upon free choice. On a daily basis, it is left with us to choose whom we will serve. That choice is a permission slip we give to God, allowing Him to fill us with power and to change us into His likeness—to transform us.

> *"As the **will of man** cooperates with **the will of God**, it becomes **omnipotent**"*
> (*Christ's Object Lessons*, p. 333).

In the battle with evil and temptation, what does this promise mean to you?

_____

_____

If we are to have any hope of eternal life, we must understand that our victory is dependent upon the yielding of our will to God. Anything less than 100 percent surrender to Him will mean disaster in the battle of overcoming evil! "The will is the governing power in the nature of man, bringing all the other faculties under its sway. The will is not the taste or the inclination, but it is the deciding power, which works in the children of men unto obedience to God, or unto disobedience. . . . The will is . . . the power of decision" (*Child Guidance*, p. 209).

➡ **Taking time with the Lord.** As a being of free will, the choice is yours. Wouldn't you like to yield your will fully to God today? Pray for God to guide you to make the right decision not only today—but every day.

> *"Our greatest desire is that you may be subjects of grace. You will never be saved against your will. You must prize salvation, and submit to be saved in the Lord's appointed way."*

---

*An Appeal to the Youth, p. 70.

Divine Appointment

"He who had conquered Satan in the wilderness of temptation
was again brought face to face with His enemy."
—Ellen G. White*

Jesus was ever about His Father's business. On this particular day He traveled across the Sea of Galilee to meet a demon-possessed man who, by his own choices, had allowed the devil to transform him into not much more than an animal. Scripture records that this individual had degenerated to the point of having perhaps thousands of demons residing within him.

In *The Desire of Ages* we're able to look at this story from a wider viewpoint of the conflict of the ages—

> "*The mind of this wretched sufferer had been darkened by Satan, but in the Savior's presence a ray of light had pierced the gloom. He was roused to long for freedom from Satan's control; but the demon resisted the power of Christ. When the man tried to appeal to Jesus for help, the evil spirit put words into his mouth, and he cried out in an agony of fear. The demoniac partially comprehended that he was in the presence of One who could set him free; but when he tried to come within reach of that mighty hand, another's will held him, another's words found utterance through him. The conflict between the power of Satan and his own desire for freedom was terrible*" (p. 255).

Despite this wretched man's inability to save himself, he still exercised choice to seek after God. Mark 5:15 records, "*They came to Jesus, and saw the one who had been demon-possessed and had the legion, sitting and clothed and in his right mind.*"

This man had been naked, so where did his clothing come from? Scripture does not say, but I believe Jesus shared His own clothing with this new child of God. What an amazing example of justification, the righteousness of God wrapped around him. And the meaning of being in his right mind? Jesus cast out every demon and shared His own mind with him—the mind of Christ *became* his mind. Sanctification—transformation—at its finest!

This was a divine encounter! What happened once the demoniac encountered Christ?

_____

_____

_____

This same Jesus is seeking an encounter with you every day.

How does this story speak to you?

_____

_____

_____

_____

_____

Can you identify one or more special divine encounters between you and your Lord that have occurred recently?

- _____
- _____
- _____

A Twenty-first-century Demoniac

A friend once shared her daughter's door-to-door witnessing experience, which perfectly illustrates that Jesus is still actively pursuing a love relationship with everyone.

The two young women had been sharing Christ in a neighborhood when they ventured upon a large frightening home with a Hurst/Oldsmobile parked in the driveway. They thought about skipping the residence altogether, but then remembered the words of their trainer: "Go to every home; don't pass by any of them!"

Mustering up every ounce of courage they could, they rang the bell. Within a heartbeat, a spiked-haired, body-pierced, black-clothed man stood before them. After gathering their wits, they invited him to sign up for Bible studies. After a moment of pause, he spoke. "Go ahead and leave the card." They gave him the card and rapidly left.

Months later at a church, a handsome young man approached the girls and said, "Hello. You might not remember me, but I'm the fellow that had the Hurst parked in the driveway. I was so unhappy with my life that I had just prayed that day that if there was a God, He would send someone. And you came!"

➡ **Read Isaiah 1:18.**

What part of this divine appointment is yours to perform—and what part is God's?

_____

_____

God is a rational being, and He asks that you be rational as well. Your part in this exchange is to respond to His appointment—to sit down with Him and discuss your life. After He explains the many pitfalls that await you if you make the journey on your own, He asks that you accept His invitation to join Him in preparation for eternity. Once you do your part and accept, His part is to clothe you and give you a right mind—His mind.

What did God share with you today?

_____

_____

_____

➡ **Taking time with the Lord.** Of particular importance is the fact that this whole process is a two-way exchange. If you are anything like me, you typically want to do much of the talking, but God has something to say too. This might seem a little odd, but I would like you to sit down in front of an empty chair and read Isaiah 55. As you read, think of God sitting in the chair and speaking to you these living words. You are encountering God, so don't rush this time with Him. Enjoy His presence. Go on; give it a try!

_____

The Desire of Ages, p. 256.

4

From Danger to Safety

Field marshal viscount "Monty" Montgomery was a revered Englishman who loved God with all of his heart. A hymnbook publisher was opening a new printing plant and invited him to be their keynote speaker. After looking over some of their hymns, he urged the publisher to rewrite several of them because he didn't think they portrayed humanity's true nature. Monty said, "We sing, 'O Paradise, . . . How I long for Thee.' But we do not really long for that. We long to stay on here a bit longer." Then he added, "I would like to see an author write 'O Paradise, . . . I have a little shop, and just as long as profits last, here I mean to stop.'"

You might recall that when King Artaxerxes gave the command and money so that Jerusalem could be restored and rebuilt, not every Jew was happy. Over time, they had established businesses and settled down to enjoy the "good life" in Babylon. When the time came to head home, only a remnant was willing to leave their old life behind.

Likewise, you and I are in danger of enjoying our captivity far too much. But be warned, terrible consequences lurk for those who cling to the things of this earth!

For years I've had, hanging on my office wall, a beautiful painting that depicts Christ overlooking Jerusalem. I love contemplating the warmth and care that it calls to mind. With tears flooding His eyes, Jesus sighs, *"O Jerusalem, Jerusalem, the one who kills the prophets and stones those who are sent to her! How often I wanted to gather your children together, as a hen gathers her chicks under her wings, but you were not willing!"* (Matt. 23:37). Oh, to be gathered under the wings of El Shaddai—our great Redeemer, Protector, and Provider!

Sin placed a barrier between Deity and humanity. It wasn't long after the Garden of Eden tragedy that God began using faithful men and women to speak on His behalf. Ever since, their job has been to admonish, warn, direct, counsel, encourage, intercede, and instruct humankind—to call us out of sin so the Father can gather us under His mighty wings of protection. They always call people from danger to safety.

Continually Calling

"Come out from among them and be separate, says the Lord.
Do not touch what is unclean, and I will receive you."
—2 Corinthians 6:17

In one of the shortest verses in the Bible, Luke 17:32, Jesus cautions us to "remember Lot's wife." **Study the account found in Genesis 13:7-12.** As the old saying goes: "The devil is in the details."

What area did Lot pick for himself and why?

_____

_____

Notice, Lot picked the land nearest the cities, which were inhabited by evil men. Can we make the same mistake as we journey on life's pathway?

Explain your answer:

_____

_____

➡ **Now read the results of Lot's decision in Genesis 19:1-38.**

What eventually happened at Sodom? Check all that apply:

☐ God saw that the evil was so great that, in order to protect humanity, the people of Sodom had to be destroyed.

☐ Lot's desire to seek the "good life" in Sodom made evil look less offensive to him.

☐ When Lot tried to get his children to leave, they mocked him.

☐ Lot's wife loved the city of Sodom more than she loved God.

☐ In hoping to secure earthly riches, Lot lost the greater part of his family.

☐ Even after leaving the big city, Lot's two remaining daughters were corrupted by its evil influence.

God's desire is to separate us from that which will ultimately cause us harm. He says, *"Let the wicked forsake his way"* (Isa. 55:7). What were the means God used to call Lot and his family from danger to safety?

_____

*"He who knows the end from the beginning, who understands our nature
and our needs—our compassionate Redeemer—saw our dangers and difficulties,
and condescended to give us timely warning and instruction
concerning our habits of life"* (Counsels on Health, p. 598).

*"Only be strong and very courageous, that you may observe to do according
to all the law which Moses My servant commanded you;
do not turn from it to the right hand or to the left,
that you may prosper wherever you go"* (Joshua 1:7).

Malachi 3:6	"Beware of false prophets."
Hebrews 13:8	There are "many false prophets."
1 John 4:1-3	"I do not change."
Matthew 7:15, 16	God is the "same yesterday, today, and forever."

Not only does God not change, Jesus warns us of false prophets in the church today. That means God has given us real prophets to guide church members in our day. Notice Paul's statement to the Ephesian church:

"[God] gave some to be apostles, some prophets, . . . for the equipping
of the saints for the work of ministry, for the edifying of the body of Christ,
till we all come to the unity of the faith and of the knowledge of the Son of God,
. . . that we should no longer be children, tossed to and fro and carried about
with every wind of doctrine, by the trickery of men, in the cunning craftiness
of deceitful plotting" (Eph. 4:11-14).

In the above text, **circle the results** of being led by God's prophets.

Just as Israel of old desired a king to rule over them rather than a prophet, we—the progressive, modern people of the global community—often find it difficult to look to a modern-day prophet—but look we must, or we will find ourselves like the church members of Matthew 7:22, 23, who will meet Christ on judgment day:

"Many will say to Me in that day, 'Lord, Lord, have we not prophesied in Your name,
cast out demons in Your name, and done many wonders in Your name?'
And then I will declare to them, 'I never knew you; depart from Me, you who practice lawlessness!'"

Rather than listening to the messengers whom God sends, some create their own messages, spawned from the human heart: *"The time will come when they will not endure sound doctrine, but according to their own desires, because they have itching ears, they will heap up for themselves teachers; and they will turn their ears away from the truth, and be turned aside to fables"* (2 Tim. 4:3, 4). They will be fully convinced that they had been doing God's will, but in the end, they will be wrong.

God sees the end from the beginning, so He knows how many apples are going to be produced from a single apple seed. The same holds true regarding your life. He yearns to guide your footsteps so you can produce a glorious harvest for yourself and for everyone you touch—from now and throughout eternity.

➡ **Fill in the blank:** *"Most assuredly, I say to you, he who _____ receives Me; and he who receives Me receives Him who sent Me"* (John 13:20).

Historically, God has delivered major prophecies to His people and then, near the time of their fulfillment, He has raised up another prophet to confirm the message, to call attention to the fact that the time is at hand.

He gave Daniel this amazing prophecy concerning the fate of Israel and the coming Messiah:

"Seventy weeks are determined for your people . . . to finish the transgression,
to make an end of sins, to make reconciliation for iniquity,
. . . and to anoint the Most Holy. Know therefore . . . that from the going forth
of the command to restore and build Jerusalem until Messiah the Prince,
there shall be seven weeks and sixty-two weeks" (Dan. 9:24, 25).

God's celestial clock ticked off the years and did not miss a beat. At the appointed time God raised up John the Baptist, who *"preached, saying, 'There comes One after me who is mightier than I, whose sandal strap I am not worthy to stoop down and loose. I indeed baptized you with water, but He will baptize you with the Holy Spirit'"* (Mark 1:7, 8).

Many more instances in the Bible reveal God's pattern of calling forth another prophet to confirm a prophecy so His people are sure to recognize it. Another one from Daniel especially comes to mind—a prophecy that stretched across time to the year 1844: *"For two thousand three hundred days; then the sanctuary shall be cleansed"* (Dan. 8:14). It was a judgment-hour message for the people of Laodicea (see Rev. 3:14).

True to form, God raised up a prophet to help His people remember it was time for the earth to be judged prior to His coming. Her name was Ellen White, and she wrote:

> *"As the third angel's message arose . . . which is to reveal the law of God to the church in its fullness and power, the prophetic gift was also immediately restored. This gift has acted a very prominent part in the . . . carrying forward of this message"* (Loma Linda Messages, p. 33).

> *"As the condition of the church and the world was opened before me, and I beheld the fearful scenes that lie just before us, I was alarmed at the outlook; and night after night, while all in the house were sleeping, I wrote out the things given me of God. I was shown the heresies which are to arise, the delusions that will prevail, the miracle-working power of Satan—the false Christs that will appear—that will deceive the greater part even of the religious world, and that would, if it were possible, draw away even the elect"* (Selected Messages, book 3, p. 114).

God has given us a prophet at the end of time to call us from danger to safety:

> *"Now is our time to prepare to meet Christ. God has given us this time, and if we use it in self-gratification instead of in helping others and honoring God, we shall come up to the judgment unprepared. In that day many will plead as an excuse that they did not know that Christ's coming was near. But the excuse will not be accepted. They did not know simply because they did not want to know. God gave them abundant opportunity for knowing, but they closed their eyes, that they might not see, and stopped their ears, that they might not hear"* (Signs of the Times, Apr. 12, 1905).

➡ **Taking time with the Lord.** Rejoice in prayer today that God's love for you runs so deep that He has not left you alone in the war against evil, nor unaware of the times in which we live, but has provided a guide to point out the temptations, pitfalls, and dangers along your pathway.

> *"For prophecy never came by the will of man, but holy men of God spoke as they were moved by the Holy Spirit."*

Do You Believe?

"And you, child, will be called the prophet of the Highest;
for you will go before the face of the Lord to prepare His ways."
—Luke 1:76

"I cannot express to you the intense desire of my soul that you should all seek the Lord most earnestly while He may be found. We are in the day of God's preparation. Let nothing be regarded as of sufficient worth to draw your minds from the work of preparing for the great day of judgment. Get ready. Let not cold unbelief hold your souls away from God, but let His love burn on the altar of your hearts."
—Ellen G. White*

This message of love and warning was written by Ellen White, a woman called by God to warn His people that Jesus' coming was imminent.

All people must now prepare their hearts and lives to receive Him. Have you received Jesus into your heart, fully and completely? Are you willing to trust Him however He leads you?

Ask God to guide you in your answer as you write it down:

_____

➡ **Read Matthew 23:37, 38.**

What did Jesus say was Israel's problem?

_____

What was the result of their actions?

_____

The children of Israel could not prosper or be gathered under the wings of the Almighty, because they continually attacked His prophets. What a sad situation! I imagine that most of the time they believed they had good cause to doubt, ignore, debase, and kill those sent by God—including Jesus.

Yet Jesus said, *"If they do not hear Moses and the prophets, neither will they be persuaded though one rise from the dead"* (Luke 16:31). In other words, they didn't believe the prophets, so they did not have a foundation to believe Jesus despite His raising Lazarus.

This was a very serious problem in Jesus' day; it is a problem in our day, too. **Why?**

_____

Neither human nature nor the wiles of the devil have changed. He is well aware of the fact that he has a much better chance of deceiving God's people if we do not heed the guidance and warnings that come through His prophets, including Ellen White.

Janene's Testimony

"At the time of my baptism, I was not fully convinced that Ellen White was a messenger of the Lord. The idea of a prophet was extremely foreign to my concept of contemporary thought and culture.

"What changed my mind? I decided to follow Jesus' counsel and became a fruit inspector [Matt. 7:20]. The more I read her writings and understood her amazing counsel, the more it became clear to me that her messages had been given to her by God. After thoroughly inspecting her writings, I realized that she was, indeed, a prophet—and I was ready to listen to God's counsel through her."

What is your position regarding Ellen White?

☐ I had her shoved down my throat as a kid and am skeptical today.

☐ I believe God sent her to warn and guide us today.

☐ I'm like Janene was; I'm not sure.

☐ I believe some of what she has written.

☐ I would like to study more of her writings.

☐ I am asking God to help me with this.

☐ Other _____.

Let's now examine Ellen White and inspect some of her fruit:

- She is the one of the most translated writers in the history of literature.
- She received approximately 2,000 visions and dreams: They varied in length from less than a minute to nearly *four hours*. During a number of her visions she was under close medical examination; she did not breathe, and her lungs were void of air. In addition, her eyes would remain open, but she wouldn't blink.

Can a human survive without oxygen for four hours?

☐ yes

☐ no

Can the human eye remain healthy when deprived of tears for hours at a time?

☐ yes

☐ no

➡ **If you aren't sure of the answers, verify the facts on a medical Web site.**

More Facts and Fruit

- During at least one vision, this small woman held up an 18-pound Bible at arm's length for more than a half hour while quoting and pointing to verses from the book held above eye level.
- Her work was one of edification, exhortation, and comfort.
- She was instrumental in her church's organizational structure.
- She received many visions calling for a publishing ministry that would encircle the globe, leading to more than 60 publishing houses, 17 literature ministry seminaries, hundreds of book centers, and tens of thousands of literature evangelists distributing literature to a world hungering for the gospel.
- Her church's health system is one of the largest in the world, comprising 173 hospitals, 216 clinics, and 132 nursing homes and retirement centers.
- Her visions and counsels regarding health reform have benefited those who follow them. Studies show that both men and women live five to 10 years longer than their peers.

My Dreams—My Focus

"My voice You shall hear in the morning, O Lord;
in the morning I will direct it to You, and I will look up."
—Psalm 5:3

"Wherever you are, be all there."
—Jim Elliot, missionary martyr

What do you want to accomplish? **List your dreams in order:**

- _____

- _____

- _____

- _____

What is the main purpose and focus of your life?

_____

_____

The apostle Paul wrote to Timothy in sorrow over the actions of one church member:

"Demas has forsaken me, having loved this present world, and has departed" (2 Tim. 4:10).

The so-called American dream is diametrically opposed to the plans of God: self-advancement, self-esteem, self-sufficiency, individualism, materialism—self, self, self. In addition, many Christians have become lulled into the concept of universalism, the popular belief that says all roads lead to eternity with God. It sounds nice, *but it's untrue!*

➡ **Read and meditate upon the following texts:**

- John 14:6
- John 10:9
- Acts 4:12
- 1 John 2:22-25

Describe the main thrust of the texts you just read:

_____

_____

According to these texts, is it possible for you to deny Jesus? If so, are you denying Him?

_____

_____

Psalm 16:11 says, *"You will show me the path of life; in Your presence is fullness of joy; at Your right hand are pleasures forevermore.*" The only pathway that leads to life is the one that involves a saving relationship with Jesus Christ.

After Jesus shared this concept with a wider group of church members, many left Him (John 6:60-67). They were not ready for the radical changes involved. Then He turned to the disciples nearest to Him and asked if they would also leave Him now that they understood the commitment involved. Peter had it right:

> "*Simon Peter answered Him, 'Lord, to whom shall we go? You have the words of eternal life'*" (John 6:68).

Adam Clarke makes this observation regarding this decisive moment in the lives of Christ's disciples—this fork in the road:

> "*With his usual zeal and readiness speaking in behalf of the whole to whom shall we go? Where shall we find a more gracious master—a more powerful Redeemer—a more suitable Savior? . . . None can teach the doctrine of salvation but thyself. . . . Reader, let me ask, whither art thou going? Has the world—the devil—the flesh—the words [of] eternal life? Art thou turning thy back upon God and Christ? For thy zealous services, what has Satan to [give] thee? Death! hell! and eternal misery! O stop! Cleave to Jesus; he will give thee that happiness which, in vain, thou seekest in the pleasures of sin.*"

The gods of the world's religions demand appeasement, yet those who worship them have no guarantee that they will ever find peace. Those who chase after idols find it's never enough. How different with the King of the universe! He came down to seek friendship with all who are willing to draw near to Him. His greatest desire is to abide with you!

Are you willing to invite Him in? **Share what is on your heart:**

_____

_____

_____

> "*I firmly believe that the moment our hearts are emptied of pride and selfishness and ambition and self-seeking and everything that is contrary to God's law, the Holy Ghost will come and fill every corner of our hearts; but if we are full of pride and conceit and ambition and self-seeking and pleasure and the world, there is no room for the Spirit of God; and I believe many a man is praying to God to fill him when he is full already with something else.*"—Dwight L. Moody.

God once used a preacher on a video to speak to my heart: "You have piled up so much of this world's goods in front of your door," he said, "that even when God does knock, you can't make it to the door to answer." These words changed my life.

Are there things of this world—"toys"—that you have piled up in front of your door that could be making it hard to hear and answer God's knock? Take a moment with God and ask Him to help you **list those things that might, or have, become a barrier between you and Him.**

- _____

- _____

- _____

- _____

> "*For after all these things the Gentiles seek. For your heavenly Father knows that you need all these things. But seek first the kingdom of God and His righteousness, and all these things shall be added to you*" (Matt. 6:32, 33).

➡ **Taking time with the Lord.** Pray this prayer: "Lord, I want nothing to come between You and me. I choose only

You! But I am incapable of overcoming my own desires and need Your help. Please do help me right now. Show me if there is anything in my life that I must change or abandon. I choose You and invite You into my life at this very moment. If there are things in front of the door, please remove them and come to me, abide in me and change me. Give me Your Holy Spirit. Fill me so I desire nothing more than You."

> *"My voice You shall hear in the morning, O Lord;*
> *in the morning I will direct it to You, and I will look up."*

Busted

"My little children, these things I write to you, so that you may not sin.
And if anyone sins, we have an Advocate with the Father,
Jesus Christ the righteous."
—1 John 2:1

Two sinners experienced dramatic encounters with Jesus. Both episodes are recorded in the Gospel of John. After their face-to-face encounters with the God of love, they were never the same again.

➧ **Take time to read, visualize, and contemplate** the events and the message Jesus delivered to these wayward children:

- John 8:2-12
- John 5:1-14

In your own words, describe what took place in each encounter:

_____

_____

_____

_____

What did Jesus command them to do?

_____

Did you notice that He did not make a suggestion? It was not a softly worded request. It was straightforward—black and white. There was no room for a misunderstanding!

➧ **Read John 8:12** again and write out what Jesus said was the key to success:

_____

Each had been leading a life of radical sin rather than a life of radical commitment to God. Jesus forgave them, but then He told them it was time to stop doing what they were doing. They had been busted, and it was time for them to go in a new direction. But how? The key to transformation is following the Light and ceasing to walk in darkness.

You might be saying, "Easier said than done," but it is possible with Jesus!

"The renewing energy must come from God. The change can be made only by the Holy Spirit. All who would be saved, high or low, rich or poor, must submit to the working of this power" (Christ's Object Lessons, p. 96).

Circle the statement or phrase contained in each of the following texts that speaks of God's desire for you to yield to Him:

"Submit to God. Resist the devil and he will flee from you" (James 4:7).

"For they being ignorant of God's righteousness, and seeking to establish their own righteousness, have not submitted to the righteousness of God" (Rom. 10:3).

*"Take My yoke upon you and learn from Me, for I am gentle and lowly in heart,
and you will find rest for your souls"* (Matt. 11:29).

*"The weapons of our warfare are not carnal but mighty in God for pulling down strongholds,
casting down arguments and every high thing that exalts itself against the knowledge of God,
bringing every thought into captivity to the obedience of Christ"* (2 Cor. 10:4, 5).

*"Who among you fears the Lord? Who obeys the voice of His Servant? Who walks in darkness
and has no light? Let him trust in the name of the Lord and rely upon his God"* (Isa. 50:10).

"Having been perfected, He became the author of eternal salvation to all who obey Him" (Heb. 5:9).

*"As obedient children, not conforming yourselves to the former lusts, . . .
but as He who called you is holy, you also be holy in all your conduct"* (1 Peter 1:14, 15).

Look over the areas you circled and share your thoughts with God regarding them by asking, *"How does this relate to me and my present circumstances—to the time I spend with God, to my family, my job, my church, and to my life in general?"*

_____

_____

_____

➡ **Taking time with the Lord.** God's greatest desire for you is for you to experience the joy of a forever friendship with Him, but your cooperation is needed. Pray that God will help you cooperate with Him in His will for your life.

{ *"My little children, these things I write to you, so that you may not sin. And if anyone sins, we have an Advocate with the Father, Jesus Christ the righteous."* }

Restored and Restoring

"As through one man's offense judgment came to all men, resulting in condemnation, even so through one Man's righteous act the free gift came to all men, resulting in justification of life."
—Romans 5:18

"None are so vile, none have fallen so low, as to be beyond the working of [God's grace]. In all who will submit themselves to the Holy Spirit a new principle of life is to be implanted; the lost image of God is to be restored in humanity."
—Ellen G. White*

Janene and I have had the privilege of visiting and exploring many of Europe's great castles. Our favorites are King Ludwig II's castles of Germany.

Over the years we discovered that many castles have been restored on the outside but are in a state of ongoing restoration inside. The restorers typically start on the outside—making everything look beautiful to attract tourists—and then continue the work of restoration on the inside as time and money permit. Every molding, every staircase, and every ornate tile is brought back to their original glory and, in some cases, even better than the original.

It's fascinating to watch the various artisans painstakingly apply sheet after sheet of gold leaf to plain-looking wooden walls, doorjambs, window casings, and more—and the lighting of one candle or the flick of a switch that causes the entire room to radiate and sparkle.

The artisans, of course, do not place new gold over old rotting wood. They start by replacing any damaged wood first. What would be the point otherwise? The rotting wood would eventually destroy the gold leaf.

Let's return to the woman who was caught in the act of adultery and brought to Christ for judgment. Instead of stoning her, as many expected Him to do, Jesus said, *"Neither do I condemn thee."* This is the merciful process known as **justification**. Jesus saw that she was repentant for her sins and forgave her, figuratively wrapping His righteousness around her. She had been restored—instantly becoming a pardoned child of the King!

But Jesus was not finished. **Read John 8:11 and write out His next five words:**

Jesus had just covered her exterior with pure gold—His righteousness. This represented her perfect standing as a child of the King. But then He instructed her to *"go and sin no more."* He moved from outside restoration to inside restoration. He began to remove the rotten wood on the inside and apply the same gold He had used on the outside. This is **sanctification**—a process that demands our full cooperation and is the work of a lifetime. You might say that the work on the outside and on the inside becomes our full "temple restoration project."

➡ **Match the process with the correct kinds of restoration:**

justification	inside restoration
sanctification	outside restoration

justification	progressive restoration
sanctification	instantaneous restoration

Justification is outside and instantaneous; sanctification is inside and progressive. We must be both justified and sanctified in order to be fit for heaven. Both are an act of amazing grace from the hands of a loving Creator.

➡ **Read Revelation 1:6, Revelation 5:10, and Revelation 3:21.**

Adam and Eve threw away their own righteousness in the garden paradise. It has since been God's work to restore His beauty in us in preparation for our role in heaven.

> *"Justification means the saving of a soul from perdition, that he may obtain sanctification, and through sanctification, the life of heaven. Justification means that the conscience, purged from dead works, is placed where it can receive the blessings of sanctification"* (*The Seventh-day Adventist Bible Commentary,* Ellen G. White Comments, vol. 7, p. 908).

Now explain justification and sanctification in your own words—as they relate to you, your salvation, and your future in heaven:

_____

Look up the following texts; if the verse speaks about justification, write a **J** in the space next to it. Write an **S** in the space if it is about sanctification.

1. Romans 5:1_____
2. Romans 3:23-25_____
3. Romans 6:4 _____
4. Romans 6:16_____
5. Romans 8:14_____†

In Romans Paul uses four chapters to explain justification and six to expound upon sanctification, leaving little doubt that God is concerned with our restoration not only on the outside, but also on the inside. He wants us to be complete in Him—lacking nothing. *"Having been set free from sin, you became slaves of righteousness"* (Rom. 6:18).

Have you repented of your sins and been set free? Have you been restored by God's covering righteousness?
☐ yes
☐ no
☐ not sure

By His power, are you allowing God to enable you to become a servant of righteousness—following His command to *"go and sin no more"*?
☐ I need to understand this process better.
☐ I'm trying.
☐ Yes, I am.
☐ Not yet, but I'm willing to seek God's help.
☐ other: _____ .

➡ **Taking time with the Lord.** In prayer, ask God to help you accept all the work He needs to do inside and outside of you to prepare you for eternity. If you are not yet willing for Him to do all the restoration He wants to do in your "temple restoration project," ask Him to make you willing to be made willing.

Christ's Object Lessons, p. 96.

†Answers: 1. J. 2. J. 3. S. 4. S. 5. S.

Radical Obedience

"Jesus came to Galilee, preaching the gospel of the kingdom of God,
and saying, 'The time is fulfilled, and the kingdom of God is at hand.
Repent, and believe in the gospel.'"
—Mark 1:14, 15

When I was growing up, the song "I Did It My Way" was very popular. It could very well be the spiritual anthem of hell. That type of thinking—doing it your own way—has absolutely no place in the Christian life. Complete surrender of our will and total obedience to Christ are the only avenues leading to heaven.

God is looking for overcomers to take to heaven with Him.

➡ **Read Revelation 2 and 3.** How many times does the word "overcomes" appear? _____.

God calls every church of every age and every follower to be overcomers! *"He who overcomes shall inherit all things, and I will be his God and he shall be My son"* (Rev. 21:7). Those who surrender their will to God and follow all He sets before them will inherit what? _____!

"Genuine conversion is transformation of character. New purposes, new moral tastes are created. Defects of character are overcome. Truth, with its sanctifying power, brings the entire man into obedience" (Testimonies to Southern Africa, p. 30).

➡ **Read Luke 9:1-3.** What was Jesus' instruction to His disciples?

_____

➡ **Read Luke 14:16-28.** What do you think it costs to be a disciple of Christ?

_____

➡ **Read Luke 14:33.** What did Jesus say the cost is?

_____

How do you think the disciples felt after hearing those words from Christ?

_____

_____

What is the key to a successful and fruitful Christian life?

_____

_____

Dwight L. Moody was going to England for an evangelistic campaign. An elderly pastor protested, "Why do we need him? He's uneducated and inexperienced! Does he think he has a monopoly on the Holy Spirit?" A younger, wiser pastor responded, "No. But the Holy Spirit has a monopoly on Mr. Moody."

God is looking to have all there is of you, but how does that become reality? How can you offer God radical obedience? (Of course, only the world calls complete submission radical. It is, in reality, normal Christian deportment.)

What are your thoughts?

_____

_____

_____

➡ **Circle the key words or phrases that reflect obedience:**

"He who draws nigh to Christ need not try to shine. As he beholds [Jesus], he catches the divine rays of light from the Sun of Righteousness, and he cannot help shining. The light that is in him shines forth in clear, bright rays, in words and works of righteousness. Christ's grace dwells in him richly. . . . He honors Christ by complete obedience" (*The Upward Look*, p. 322).

The key to heaven is found in a relationship with Jesus! We must draw near to the One who overcame on our behalf. We must rely upon His power to shine from within us.

"Jesus can supply your every need, if you will look to Him and trust in Him. As you behold Him, you will be charmed with the riches of the glory of His divine love. The idolatrous love of things that are seen will be superseded by a higher and better love for things that are imperishable and precious. You may contemplate eternal riches until your affections are bound to things above, and you may be an instrument in directing others to set their affections on heavenly treasures" (*Review and Herald*, June 23, 1896).

➡ **Taking time with the Lord.** Andrew Murray said, "May not a single moment of my life be spent outside the light, love, and joy of God's presence and not a moment without the entire surrender of myself as a vessel for Him to fill full of His Spirit and His love." Will you choose to be His vessel today? Ask God in prayer for His help.

> *"Jesus came to Galilee, preaching the gospel of the kingdom of God, and saying, 'The time is fulfilled, and the kingdom of God is at hand. Repent, and believe in the gospel.'"*

Hidden Truth!

"These things I have spoken to you, that My joy may remain in you,
and that your joy may be full."
—John 15:11

"The degree of blessing enjoyed by any man will correspond exactly with the
completeness of God's victory over him."
—A. W. Tozer

Dwight L. Moody once held up a glass and asked, "How can I get the air out of this glass?" One man told him to suck it out with a pump. Moody replied, "That would create a vacuum and shatter the glass." After numerous other suggestions, Moody picked up a pitcher of water and filled the glass. "There," he said. "All the air is now removed." He went on to explain that victory in the Christian life is not accomplished by " 'sucking out a sin here and there,' but by being filled with the Holy Spirit."

The devil has kept this truth hidden from God's people: God does not want Christians who are clean on the outside only; He wants you clean on the inside, too!

Cliff Richard said, "The more we depend on God, the more dependable we find He is." Victory over sin is possible when you surrender your will fully and completely to God. At that moment the Holy Spirit takes up residence (abides) in your temple (your life) and provides you overcoming power. You can depend on God to act when you ask!

Have you ever experienced the dependability of God's power in your life to separate you from sin?

☐ No.
☐ I'm not sure.
☐ Yes! It is wonderful!

If you have experienced His overcoming power, explain how it happened. If not, why not?

_____

_____

God is all-powerful. If you invite Him to abide in you, then you have invited Victory to take control of you. It's not about you; it's all about God. Can you do it? No! Can I do it? No! But when you allow the Holy Spirit to dwell in you, you will not lose.

List any instances in the New Testament in which Jesus ran up against a trial, temptation, problem, or demon . . . and lost:

1. _____

2. _____

3. _____

That's right! There isn't even a single instance in which Jesus did not firmly beat the devil or his minions, human or otherwise. God *always* wins! Follow Him, and victory is yours—guaranteed!

What can you do to ensure that you experience Divinity's life-changing power?

_____

An angel appeared to Ellen White in a vision on June 27, 1850: "My accompanying angel said, 'Time is almost finished. Do you reflect the lovely image of Jesus as you should?' . . . Said the angel, 'Get ready, get ready, get ready. Ye will have to die a greater death to the world than ye have ever yet died'" (*Early Writings*, p. 64).

Wow! Now imagine an angel materializing in your room at this very moment and making that statement *to you*. **Ponder the gravity of the situation and then write out what you would say to your angel and why you would say it.**

_____

_____

_____

> "There are some who seem to be always seeking for the heavenly pearl. But they do not make an entire surrender of their wrong habits. They do not die to self that Christ may live in them" (*Christ's Object Lessons*, p. 118).

What can we do? Here are wonderful promises packed with power and potential—

> "As the will of man cooperates with the will of God, it becomes omnipotent. Whatever is to be done at His command may be accomplished in His strength. All His biddings are enablings" (*Christ's Object Lessons*, p. 333).

> "When you yield up your will to Christ, your life is hid with Christ in God. It is allied to the power which is above all principalities and powers. You have a strength from God that holds you fast to His strength; and a new life, even the life of faith, is possible to you" (*My Life Today*, p. 318).

➥ **Taking time with the Lord.** As you pray today, consider your potential to be an overcomer when you and Omnipotence become one!

{
"*These things I have spoken to you,
that My joy may remain in you, and that your
joy may be full.*"
}

6

The View From Above

"But those who wait on the Lord shall renew their strength;
they shall mount up with wings like eagles, they shall run and not be weary,
they shall walk and not faint."
—*Isaiah 40:31*

My work requires a great deal of travel, so I spend a lot of time at airports and in airplanes. I normally choose an aisle seat on my flights, but on occasion I'll take a window seat so I can enjoy the amazing views. As I'm elevated far above the clouds, vast snow-covered mountain ranges, expansive fields with color patterns that dazzle the senses, and crops, lakes, dams, and forests—the list is almost endless—all vie for my attention.

Of course, the view is very different when standing at the base of a massive dam looking up at its gigantic concrete walls, as opposed to flying over that dam, the lake it holds, and the extensive forest-covered mountain range that contains it all.

My point is simply this: In the same way that flying over our world at high altitude offers a new perspective, so it can be when studying the Bible.

So all this week you will view Matthew 5 through 10 from altitude—high above the normal elevation you might normally see them—offering you a look at perhaps never-before-seen panoramas and vistas.

"Ladies and gentlemen, the cabin door is now closed. Please bring your seats to their upright and locked positions, stow all tray tables, turn off all electronics, and enjoy your flight."

The Outward to the Inward

Matthew 5

The grassy slope overlooking the tranquil Sea of Galilee was bathed in sunshine. It was a beautiful day. People had come from far and wide to hear the humble Teacher share words of life. Their time spent with the Son of God would be like no other they had experienced before.

Jesus' message, dubbed the "Sermon on the Mount," has radically changed lives ever since. You can read sacred writings from the world over—from the Bhagavad Gita to the Koran—and never encounter anything else like it! It has changed drunkards into pious souls and thieves into trustworthy men and women. It has changed the most horrific sinners into saints.

➥ **Read Matthew 5:2-11.** First, seek God in prayer and ask Him to guide your study.

What word is repeated over and over? _____. Some Bible versions say *"Happy"*; others say *"Blessed."* Either one is correct.

These statements were a radical departure from the thinking of the day. Jesus was saying that God pronounces blessings on certain life directions, but the people believed that the source of happiness was found in mirth, wealth, honor, and freedom from persecution. Jesus said, "None of the above."

Do you believe He had it right?
- ☐ yes
- ☐ no
- ☐ undecided

It is often the case that people are the happiest—even in poverty, sickness, and persecution—when Jesus is walking arm in arm with them.

I attended grammar school and high school with a fellow by the name of Larry. He and I were always in competition over everything, but he was always better than I was. He went to college on a basketball scholarship and, while there, gave his life to Christ. Sadly, multiple sclerosis ended his college days early and, eventually, his life. But before he died, he said to me that he believed he would have never gotten the disease if he had not accepted Christ. I asked him if he was sorry he had done so. He answered effortlessly, "Jim, I would not change a thing!"

➥ **Do you have that kind of hold upon God?** If not, why not ask God now to help you? If you do, thank Him in prayer for giving you strength and faith.

Next, Jesus struck at the foundation of all the supposed righteousness of the day, saying, *"Unless your righteousness exceeds the righteousness of the scribes and Pharisees, you will by no means enter the kingdom of heaven"* (Matt. 5:20).

This left the astonished crowd asking, "If even our church leaders aren't going to make it to heaven, what hope do we have?" Jesus then moved their thoughts from the outward life, with all of its display, to the inward heart—a place they had not gone before in their thinking.

➡ **Read Matthew 5:21, 22.** Fill in the word, inward or outward, that describes the intent of the text:

Verse 21 _____

Verse 22 _____

➡ **Read Matthew 5:27, 28.** Fill in the word, inward or outward, that describes the intent of the text:

Verse 27 _____

Verse 28 _____

In these verses Jesus began to tear away at the human-made traditions of the rabbis. He sought to call them back to God's plan of a changed heart. He didn't want them to just look good on the outside. *"As he thinks in his heart, so is he"* (Prov. 23:7).

Which statement best describes your situation?

☐ I've never thought much about making inward or outward changes in my life.

☐ I tried to make changes, but I just couldn't.

☐ God is making those changes in my life so long as I surrender to Him.

☐ other: _____

As the saying goes, Jesus next "went from preaching to meddling," telling the crowd, *"Therefore you shall be perfect, just as your Father in heaven is perfect"* (Matt. 5:48).

Do you think you can accomplish the task of being perfect on your own? Explain:

_____

> *"God's ideal for His children is higher than the highest human thought can reach. 'Be ye therefore perfect, even as your Father which is in heaven is perfect.' This command is a promise. The plan of redemption contemplates our complete recovery from the power of Satan. Christ always separates the contrite soul from sin. He came to destroy the works of the devil, and He has made provision that the Holy Spirit shall be imparted to every repentant soul, to keep him from sinning"* (The Desire of Ages, p. 311).

Who accomplishes the monumental task of changing you and making you perfect?

☐ I do.

☐ Nobody can.

☐ I am too much of a sinner.

☐ God can do it!

☐ It's a combination of God and me.

You can do nothing to change your life—not any part of it—but God can. *It's all about God!* What He needs is your permission to give the Holy Spirit entrance into your heart, and He'll change you as promised!

➡ **Taking time with the Lord.** Will you allow Him to enter your heart and change you completely? Take time in prayer now to share with Him what's on your heart.

> *"But those who wait on the Lord shall renew their strength; they shall mount up with wings like eagles, they shall run and not be weary, they shall walk and not faint."*

Not Done Yet

"Let the wicked forsake his way, and the unrighteous man his thoughts;
let him return to the Lord, and He will have mercy on him;
and to our God, for He will abundantly pardon."
—Isaiah 55:7

Matthew 6 and 7

There are no breaks in the action between Matthew 5, 6, and 7. The people were transfixed because no one had ever taught a message like this man. Jesus did not miss a beat, however, slamming the hypocrites who used religion only as a display. (See Matt. 6:1-8.)

As Jesus spoke, these questions were undoubtedly raised in the minds of His audience: "How can I ever become what You have asked me to become? How can I do what You say I need to do to be saved?" Good questions! How would you answer them?

➡ **Read Matthew 6:9-13** to discover the right answer. What is the key to overcoming and doing all Jesus commanded them—and you?

_____

The radical changes Christ asks you to make cannot be made without you connecting into the Power Source. The connecting mechanism is prayer.

*"Why should the sons and daughters of God be reluctant to pray, **when prayer is the key** in the hand of faith to unlock heaven's storehouse, where are treasured the boundless resources of Omnipotence?"* (*Steps to Christ*, p. 94).

Are you connecting into the Power Source on a daily basis? If so, how long do you usually spend in time with God?

_____

Jesus says our priorities must change. We must shift our focus. Our time, our energy, our talents must be upon the eternal and not upon the transitory!

"Lay up for yourselves treasures in heaven, where neither moth nor rust destroys and where thieves do not break in and steal. For where your treasure is, there your heart will be also" (Matt. 6:20, 21).

➡ **Take a few minutes and review your goals and priorities,** the use of your time, talents, and focus. Do you sense anything in your life that God wants you to adjust or change? Be honest with yourself and God:

_____

_____

In verses 22-24 Jesus next presented major contrasts between the forces of good and the forces of evil. The following is my summation of those verses. **Give thought and consider these statements in relation to you and God:**
- Light and darkness cannot coexist in the same body.

- As you behold, so you become.
- No man can serve two masters.
- Jesus is the light of the world.

Jesus sums up Matthew 6 by saying:
- I take care of the birds and the lilies, so don't worry about the "other stuff." The lost wander the world worrying about this stuff, but not My children!
- Seek a life-transforming relationship with Me, and I will take care of you.

➡ **Read Matthew 7:7-11.**

Jesus wasn't finished! He promised that the God of the universe has provided you with the keys to eternal happiness, peace, and contentment—all beginning in this life. *"Ask, and it will be given to you; seek, and you will find; knock, and it will be opened to you"* (verse 7).

But remember, the ground rules to receive answers were set up in the previous verses. Jesus then shared the sad truth regarding how many people will actually follow His road map to eternal happiness:

➡ **Fill in the missing words:**

"Enter by the _____, for wide is the gate and broad is the way that leads to destruction, and there are _____ who go in by it. Because _____ is the gate and difficult is the way which leads to _____, and there are _____ who find it" (verses 13, 14).

As the church members of Jesus' day were sitting with their mouths wide open after this shocking revelation, Jesus dropped yet another bomb:

"Not everyone who says to Me, 'Lord, Lord,' shall enter the kingdom of heaven, but he who does the will of My Father in heaven. Many will say to Me in that day, 'Lord, Lord, have we not prophesied in Your name, cast out demons in Your name, and done many wonders in Your name?' And then I will declare to them, 'I never knew you; depart from Me, you who practice lawlessness!'" (verses 21-23).

Jesus went on to say that the only ones who will find the narrow way are those who build on the Rock by doing His will and following His ways. The rest will be washed away in a flood of evil.

"So it was, when Jesus had ended these sayings, that the people were astonished at His teaching, for He taught them as one having authority, and not as the scribes" (verses 28, 29).

Perhaps you also have been astonished to learn that Jesus requires complete obedience. Not even church members who work miracles will necessarily make it, but only those who do God's will!

"Jesus died, not to save man in his sins, but from his sins. Man is to leave the error of his ways, to follow the example of Christ, to take up his cross and follow Him, denying self, and obeying God at any cost" (*Testimonies for the Church*, vol. 4, p. 251).

Don't become discouraged. Remember, it's all about God—and all He is looking for are those who have a willing heart to join Him. Are you willing to have God change you today?

☐ Yes.

☐ No.

☐ I'm not sure.

➧ **Taking time with the Lord.** Pray these words: "Lord, I believe—help my unbelief. Change me and make me willing to be made willing. I choose to follow You regardless of my life's circumstances and problems. I do trust You. Help me to trust You more fully than I ever have before. I do love You and ask You to help my love to grow. May I see evidence of Your love for me in a special way. Give me spiritual eyes to discern spiritual things. May I be a blessing to someone today as I walk hand in hand with You. In Jesus' name, amen."

{ *"Let the wicked forsake his way, and the unrighteous man his thoughts; let him return to the Lord, and He will have mercy on him; and to our God, for He will abundantly pardon."* }

The Devil's Onslaught

"Your faith should not be in the wisdom of men but in the power of God."
—1 Corinthians 2:5

Matthew 8 and 9

Over the past two days we've covered three days of Jesus' teachings delivered on the mountainside. When He finished teaching, He walked down the mountain. But multitudes followed Him because they had to obtain the answer to this burning question: "How can I ever do what You have asked when I have no power?"

Before we walk in the footsteps of Jesus down the mountain, let's go back to the Garden of Eden for a moment. Genesis 3:15 speaks of the power needed to do all He has said we must do: *I will put enmity between you and the woman, and between your seed and her Seed.* After the Fall of humanity, God did not leave humans helpless but provided a source of power to overcome the devil's temptations.

Choose the word(s) that best describes "enmity":
- ☐ hostility
- ☐ antagonism
- ☐ animosity
- ☐ rancor
- ☐ antipathy
- ☐ animus

Every word here describes enmity. In the person of the Holy Spirit, God will give you hostility *against* temptations, antagonism toward evil, and so on. When you invite God into your life, *you have invited a repelling force for every demonic advance!*

> "*Human beings were a new and distinct order. . . . They were to live in close communion with heaven, receiving power from the Source of all power*" (*Sons and Daughters of God*, p. 7).

Let's now continue our journey into Matthew by looking at chapters 8 and 9. The peaceful time on the mountain is gone, and the war between good and evil is heating up. **Look at each of Christ's encounters with Satan and list what the encounter was about and the result. I will give you the first two:**

Matthew 8:2, 3: **Cleansed the leper.** God can make us clean no matter how rotten we are.

Verses 5-13: **Centurion's servant was healed long-distance.** God can do anything.

Verses 14, 15: _____

Verses 16, 17: _____

Verses 23-27: _____

Verses 28-34: _____

Matthew 9:1-8: _____

Next, in verse 9, Jesus called Matthew to follow Him. What was his response? How quickly did he respond? **Compare your response to the call of Jesus to Matthew's response:**

_____

Continue as above:

Verses 20-22: _____

Verses 23-25: _____

Verses 27-29: _____

Verses 32, 33: _____

Verses 35, 36: _____

Do you see how Jesus overcame *every* mountain—human problem—that Satan put in front of Him? The devil threw everything at Christ, but nothing caused Him to falter.

> *"When He saw the multitudes, He was moved with compassion for them,*
> *because they were weary and scattered, like sheep having no shepherd"* (Matt. 9:36).

➡ **Taking time with the Lord.** Aren't you happy that your Shepherd loves you so very much? He is well able to take care of every single need you have. As you pray, thank God for His love, mercy, and kindness. Ask Him to help you overcome every trial in your life with His unending power.

{ *"Your faith should not be in the wisdom of men but in the power of God."* }

Power

"To those who are called, both Jews and Greeks,
Christ [is] the power of God and the wisdom of God."
—1 Corinthians 1:24

Matthew 10, Part 1

Here are two inspiring statements that I don't want you to miss:

"Christ's followers are to look upon Satan as a conquered foe. . . . 'Behold,' He said, 'I give unto you power . . . over all the power of the enemy" (*The Ministry of Healing*, p. 94).

"Give me 100 men that hate nothing but sin, and love Jesus Christ, and we'll shake England for God." —*John Wesley.*

➡ **Read Matthew 10:1.**

What did Jesus give to His followers?

_____

What were the results?

_____

Jesus called His followers to His side and gave them power. In Matthew 10:1, Luke 9:1, and Luke 10:17 we discover that Jesus conferred upon them two different types of power. One power was *dunamis,* which is where our English word for dynamite is derived—it's explosive power! The other power is *exousia,* meaning authority.

As the Creator of the universe and ruler of all, God has the authority to command! Both His authority and explosive power are combined to defeat the devil and his evil angels. That's why, when the 70 followers of Christ returned, they were so joyful—*"even the demons are subject to us in Your name"* (Luke 10:17).

List the problems and the sins you are presently experiencing in life. If you don't wish to list them, do so in your mind.

_____

_____

All of God's power is ready to help you with those situations, sins, and problems as you commit to serve Him fully!

➡ **Read 2 Chronicles 14:1-15.** What did God do for Asa?

_____

God will fight for you, too. You are not left to battle the devil on your own! But remember, Asa was determined to follow God at all costs.

At one point the Jews were trying to trip Jesus up by pounding Him with trick questions, when He finally replied, *"Are you not therefore mistaken, because you do not know the Scriptures nor the power of God?"* (Mark 12:24). It's true! The Bible continually speaks of the power of God to defeat evil everywhere it is found.

➡ **Write your name in the blank space below,** because as His follower, this promise is given by God directly to you:

"Christ's followers are to look upon Satan as a conquered foe. . . . 'Behold,' He said, 'I give unto _____ power . . . over all the power of the enemy."

Romans 8:31 asks, *"What then shall we say to these things? If God is for us, who can be against us?"* **How would you answer the question?**

_____

What sins and problems in your life are bigger than God?

_____

_____

I sure hope you left that section blank!

➡ **Write your name in the following blank space:**

"Finally, _____, be strong in the Lord and in the power of His might. Put on the whole armor of God, that you may be able to stand against the wiles of the devil" (Eph. 6:10, 11).

Before Jesus departed earth, He said to His followers, *"You shall receive power when the Holy Spirit has come upon you"* (Acts 1:8). This very same Holy Spirit is seeking entrance into your life, resulting in devil-defeating power that will enable you to become an overcomer!

➡ **Write your name in all the spaces provided below.** They are all incredible promises of God to you personally:

"_____ can do all things through Christ" (Phil. 4:13).

"As the will of _____ cooperates with the will of God, it becomes omnipotent. Whatever is to be done at His command may be accomplished in His strength. All His biddings are enablings" (Christ's Object Lessons, p. 333).

"God is _____ strength and power, and He makes _____ way perfect" (2 Sam. 22:33).

"And do not lead _____ into temptation, but deliver _____ from the evil one. For Yours is the kingdom and the power, and the glory forever" (Matt. 6:13).

➡ **Taking time with the Lord.** Spend time in prayer thanking God for His promises to you. Thank Him for His gift of all-sufficient power to defeat the devil and give you complete victory through Him no matter what your sins, trials, and temptations might be at this time in your life.

> *"To those who are called, both Jews and Greeks, Christ [is] the power of God and the wisdom of God."*

Fear Not

"Fear not, for I am with you; be not dismayed, for I am your God.
I will strengthen you, yes, I will help you,
I will uphold you with My righteous right hand."
—Isaiah 41:10

"We have a God who delights in impossibilities."
—Billy Sunday

Matthew 10, Part 2

In the King James Version of Matthew 10:26 and 28, Jesus says, "Do not fear." Because we live in the quagmire of this sin-drenched world, it is sometimes difficult to see how victory can be ours—until, that is, we begin looking at the size of God. You see, the size of your God determines the success of your transformation journey into the Promised Land.

God desired to lead Israel into Canaan, the Promised Land, which He said was "flowing with milk and honey" (see Num. 13:27). When Israel reached the borders, Moses sent scouts into the country, and the report came back: It was everything God said it was. But just as the anticipation was building, 10 of the spies started grumbling, faithlessly declaring, *"Nevertheless the people who dwell in the land are strong; the cities are fortified and very large; moreover we saw the descendants of Anak [giants] there"* (verse 28).

As a trusted follower of the Lord and one of only two faithful spies, Caleb attempted to calm the fears of the unbelieving. *"Let us go up at once and take possession, for we are well able to overcome it"* (verse 30).

The devil, working through the mob's unrestrained groupthink, continued to call the power of God and His promises into question. Once doubt and fear were unleashed, it knew no bounds in the minds of the unsanctified multitude! *"The land through which we have gone . . . is a land that devours its inhabitants, and all the people whom we saw in it are men of great stature. . . . We were like grasshoppers in our own sight"* (verses 32, 33).

In the next moment the entire faithless church began to weep uncontrollably and wished they could return to their homes of captivity in Egypt.

➡ **Answer the following by circling true or false:**

true / false: All of God's promises are to be believed.

true / false: You can't blame Israel for getting nervous about giants.

true / false: If God says it, I believe it.

true / false: When we commit our lives fully to God, we have nothing to fear.

true / false: There are some things in life that God has little or no control over.

true / false: Perfect love in God casts out all fear.

In your own words, identify the real problems Israel had in taking God at His word and moving forward in faith to possess the land of Canaan:

_____

_____

How big is your God? Do you think there is a giant in your life that He cannot deal with? Share your thoughts:

_____

_____

> *"If we take Christ for our guide, He will lead us safely along the narrow way. The road may be rough and thorny; the ascent may be steep and dangerous; there may be pitfalls upon the right hand and upon the left; we may have to endure toil in our journey; when weary, when longing for rest, we may have to toil on; when faint, we may have to fight; when discouraged, we may be called upon to hope; but with Christ as our Guide we shall not lose the path to immortal life, we shall not fail to reach the desired haven at last"* (Our Father Cares, p. 134).

In order to be led safely along the pathway, you must be willing to surrender all of yourself to God and to adjust your life to do whatever He asks of you. If you are willing to allow all the wonderworking power of God to possess, control, and transform you, share your feelings with Him now:

_____

_____

> *"Through the right exercise of the will, an entire change may be made in the life. By yielding up the will to Christ, we ally ourselves with divine power"* (The Ministry of Healing, p. 176).

Rewrite the preceding statement in your own words:

_____

_____

➡ **Now read Mark 4:36-40 and answer the following questions:**

Was the boat full of water and about ready to sink? _____

Did the disciples have good cause to be fearful? _____

Did Jesus ever leave them alone? _____

Did Jesus calm the raging waters? _____

Why did Jesus say they had no faith? _____

➡ **Insert your name in the promise below:**

> *"Fear not, _____, for I am with you; be not dismayed, for I am your God. I will strengthen you. Yes, I will help you, I will uphold you with My righteous right hand. . . . For I, the Lord your God, will hold your right hand, saying to you, 'Fear not, _____, I will help you'"* (Isa. 41:10-13).

Do you sense Jesus saying something to you today? If so, what?

_____

_____

➡ **Taking time with the Lord.** Romans 8:31 says, *"What then shall we say to these things? If God is for us, who can be against us?"* Take time in prayer right now to thank God for His strength in your life. If you do not believe you have His strength, ask the Lord to give His strength as you commit all of yourself to Him and His merciful love. He is willing and able to give you all the power you need to start living a transformed life!

7

Heavenly-minded

A young man threw open the church doors, bounded outside, and went skipping and singing down the street. An older fellow saw the display and asked the young man, "Have you lost your mind?"

"Why, yes, I have, sir " was his courteous reply. "I've got the mind of Christ now!"

Up to this point, you've studied the desire of God to call you from danger to safety through His prophets, the need for radical change and commitment to the Lord, and the dynamite power and authority of God to accomplish all that He asks of you. Now it's time to apply what you have learned so that your transformation process can kick into high gear.

Here's an interesting thought:

"Contrary to popular opinion, sin is not what you want to do but can't; it is what you should not do because it will hurt you—and hurt you bad. . . . God is not a policeman; He is a Father concerned about His children. When a child picks up a snake and the father says, 'Put that down right this minute!' the child thinks he's losing a toy. The fact is, he is not losing a toy; he is losing a snake" (Steve Brown, in *Key Life*, July-August 1994).

Transformation is the process of joining God in the work of getting rid of the serpent, called Satan, from your life. I like to call it the temple restoration project; that is, restoring the heart and mind of Christ in your life.

To implement the process, God needs you to turn over the controls of your life to Him. As someone wisely said: "If God is your copilot, then it's time to switch seats." He needs to be the pilot!

Christ, our example, emptied Himself of His own will on every matter and took up the will of the Father. By joining God in the same manner, you will be forming a partnership with the Godhead that will last for eternity.

May this be a special week for you as you strive to draw nearer to God than you have ever been before. Great blessings await you!

Behold the Man

"The Word became flesh and dwelt among us, and we beheld His glory,
the glory as of the only begotten of the Father, full of grace and truth."
—John 1:14

"Then came Jesus forth wearing the crown of thorns, and the purple robe.
And Pilate said unto them, 'Behold the man!'"
—Ellen G. White*

"As you behold Christ, self will sink into insignificance, and you will be changed into
his image, 'from glory to glory, even as by the Spirit of the Lord.'"
—Ellen G. White†

➡ **Arrange the following** in the order they normally occur in the life of the Christian—I filled in the first one for you:

Behold Him   No. 1

Obey Him   _____

Know Him   _____

Love Him   _____

Believe Him   _____

Trust Him   _____

A hard-and-fast rule of the universe is that by beholding we become changed. You cannot help falling in love with Jesus when you first see Him, and once you do, you will believe what He tells you. Once you start believing what He says, you will trust Him, and if you trust Him, you will obey Him. The key is to first behold, which will enable you to know Him intimately.

Ellen White shares the best way to accomplish this:

"It would be well to spend a thoughtful hour each day reviewing the life of Christ from the manger to Calvary. We should take it point by point, and let the imagination vividly grasp each scene, especially the closing ones of his earthly life. By thus contemplating his teachings and sufferings, and the infinite sacrifice made by him for the redemption of the race, we may strengthen our faith, quicken our love, and become more deeply imbued with the spirit that sustained our Saviour. If we would be saved at last, we must learn the lesson of penitence and faith at the foot of the cross" (*Gospel Workers*, p. 246).

1. How much time do you spend reviewing the life of Christ each day?

   _____

2. Would you like to spend more time? If so, how much?

   _____

3. Are you ready to commit to spending that amount of time with the Lord each day?

   _____

4. What adjustments do you need to make in your life to accomplish this?

_____

➡️ **Go back to Ellen White's counsel and underline the statements that indicate what happens to you when you behold Christ.**

In order to strengthen your faith, quicken your love, and become more deeply imbued with the Spirit, you must increase your time beholding the matchless beauty of Christ. Choosing to do so is the first step up the transformation ladder. Even the Roman centurion discovered that spending time with God is life-changing:

> *"When the centurion . . . saw that He cried out like this and breathed*
> *His last, he said, 'Truly this Man was the Son of God!'"* (Mark 15:39).

➡️ **In the following statement, circle what Jesus can do for you. Then underline the changes that will take place in your life as you study the matchless charms of Christ.**

> *"Jesus can supply your every need, if you will look to Him and trust in Him. As you behold Him, you will be charmed with the riches of the glory of His divine love. The idolatrous love of things that are seen will be superseded by a higher and better love for things that are imperishable"* (Lift Him Up, p. 360).

> *"He who sins is of the devil, for the devil has sinned from the beginning. For this purpose the Son of God was manifested, that He might destroy the works of the devil"* (1 John 3:8).

What was the reason Jesus was revealed?

_____

This matches perfectly with Christ's words recorded in John 12:32: *"And I, if I am lifted up from the earth, will draw all peoples to Myself."* If you seek to be drawn to all that is good, pure, holy, righteous, and sinless—look at Jesus!

Select all that apply to you:

☐ I have the opportunity right now to form a character for eternity.
☐ I can work on my relationship with Christ anytime.
☐ By beholding Him, I will change into His image.
☐ There are other aspects of my life that take up my time.
☐ Eternity is not far away, so I must be about my Father's business.
☐ other: _____

Underline or circle the character changes in the following statements that you want God to accomplish in you:

> *"It is by beholding Jesus, . . . by contemplating Jesus, that you will see the offensive character of sin, of selfishness, or hardness of heart, and you will do the very thing that God requires you to do, and that you have not yet done. You will put away all self—self-importance, self-love, self-esteem, envy, evil-surmising, and jealousy, and plead for the Holy Spirit to come into your hearts and abide with you. As you taste and see that the Lord is good, you will hunger and thirst after more of the Holy Spirit, and will make an entire surrender of your will and your way, your plans and ideas, to God, and will keep the way of the Lord. Your words and deportment must be guarded"* (Youth's Instructor, Jan. 3, 1895).

> *"Looking unto Jesus we obtain brighter and more distinct views of God, and by beholding we become changed. Goodness, love for our fellow men, becomes our natural instinct. We develop a character that is the counterpart of the divine character. Growing into His likeness, we enlarge our capacity for knowing God. More and more we enter into*

fellowship with the heavenly world, and we have continually increasing power to receive the riches of the knowledge and wisdom of eternity" (*Christ's Object Lessons*, p. 355).

Rewrite the promise in this final quote into your own words:

_____

_____

_____

_____

_____

➡ **Taking time with the Lord.** Pray over the preceding promises. Ask God to speak to you regarding your present spiritual condition and to help you take time to behold Jesus every day so that you can begin the transformation process.

> *"The Word became flesh and dwelt among us, and we beheld His glory, the glory as of the only begotten of the Father, full of grace and truth."*

* Youth's Instructor, Feb. 1, 1900.

† *Youth's Instructor,* Sept. 9, 1897.

Falling in Love

"God demonstrates His own love toward us,
in that while we were still sinners, Christ died for us."
—Romans 5:8

"To say that I am made in the image of God is to say that
love is the reason for my existence, for God is love."
—Thomas à Kempis

As the hymn says: He gets "sweeter as the days go by." Because God is the God of love, He has the desire and capacity to make you joyful beyond words.

What did you experience when you first fell in love with someone? I'm guessing that person was all you could think about, all you could focus on. Everything and everyone else became secondary to the budding relationship.

Falling in love with Jesus will be far more intense. It brings great peace into the life. It is wonderfully rewarding and fulfilling, superseding every earthly relationship. Here are a few examples of the love-hunger and joy that will be found in your relationship with Christ:

"O God, You are my God; early will I seek You; my soul thirsts for You; my flesh longs for You in a dry and thirsty land where there is no water. So I have looked for You in the sanctuary, to see Your power and Your glory. Because Your lovingkindness is better than life, my lips shall praise You. Thus I will bless You while I live; I will lift up my hands in Your name. My soul shall be satisfied as with marrow and fatness, and my mouth shall praise You with joyful lips. When I remember You on my bed, I meditate on You in the night watches. Because You have been my help . . . in the shadow of Your wings I will rejoice" (Ps. 63:1-7).

"My soul longs, yes, even faints for the courts of the Lord; my heart and my flesh cry out for the living God" (Ps. 84:2).

➡ **Go back over these texts and circle the areas that convey desire or longing. Then underline the areas that signify fulfillment.**

Waylon B. Moore said, "Many of you have put a period mark by your commitment. You need to erase that period and let God lead you further—now!" Are you experiencing the hunger, the passion, and the desire to know God better?

☐ Yes, I am. I want to know God better than I ever have before.
☐ I'm beginning to.
☐ I want to.
☐ Only a little.
☐ I'm not sure.
☐ other: _____

The following statement pulls back the spiritual veil and offers us a unique glimpse into the human condition:

"In heaven it is said by the ministering angels: The ministry which we have been commissioned to perform we have done. We pressed back the army of evil angels. We sent brightness and light into the souls of men, quickening their memory of the love of God expressed in Jesus. We attracted their eyes to the cross of Christ. Their hearts were deeply moved by a sense of the sin that crucified the Son of God. They were convicted. They saw the steps to be taken in conversion; they felt the power of the gospel; their hearts were made tender as they saw the sweetness of the love of God. They beheld the beauty of the character of Christ.

"But with the many it was all in vain. They would not surrender their own habits and character. They would not put off the garments of earth in order to be clothed with the robe of heaven. Their hearts were given to covetousness. They loved the associations of the world more than they loved their God" (*Christ's Object Lessons*, p. 318).

List four impediments that cause many to miss out on the joy of falling in love with Jesus:

1. _____
2. _____
3. _____
4. _____

Are you clinging to any of these things, causing you to miss out on a deeper relationship with the Lord? If you haven't made Jesus your first passion, *now is the time to do so!*

It scares me to look back on the "second chance" period in my life and think that my self-importance, television, and worldliness almost caused me to miss out on the most exciting and joyful relationship I have ever experienced, a relationship that gets sweeter as the days go by!

➡ **Read Luke 24:50.**

While on a tour through Israel, I went to the top of the Mount of Olives. A guide pointed out the Dome of the Ascension and said, "From that spot, Jesus ascended to heaven." But Scripture says something else—He went to Bethany, over the other side of the mountain.

Although Scripture does not say why Jesus went there, I think I know. Who lived in Bethany? Martha, Mary, and Lazarus—Jesus' friends. I believe He went to say goodbye to those He was closest to.

Here's something to think about. Thousands upon thousands of people crowded around Jesus continually, pushing, shoving, and wanting something from Him, but how many wanted to be His friend? Not many. Was it because Jesus was aloof? Was it because He was hard to befriend? *No!* Instead, they all wanted something material from Jesus but were unwilling to invest their own time and energy into creating a close relationship.

Jesus desires to become your very best friend. Are you desperate for Him? If you are more willing to have a relationship with Him than you are with football, Facebook, food, or anything else, you *will* realize the desires of your heart!

➡ **Taking time with the Lord.** In prayer, share with Jesus what's on your heart at this time. If you so desire, write it out below:

_____
_____
_____
_____
_____

Mind Transplant

"I will give you a new heart and put a new spirit within you;
I will take the heart of stone out of your flesh and give you a heart of flesh."
—Ezekiel 36:26

"When the will of man comes across the will of God, one of them has to die."
—Unknown

If you've ever had a roommate, you'll recognize this phenomenon: Once they move in and the days go by, there might be some speech patterns that emerge alike between the two. They might even share some of the same eating habits and mannerisms.

This metamorphosis also holds true for married couples. It has been said that couples will even eventually begin to look alike, and scientists have conducted studies that lend credence to this idea. After all, God said that two *"shall become one flesh"* (Gen. 2:24).

This is what happens spiritually to the Christian who falls in love with Jesus and spends more and more time getting to know Him better! Hence, the apostle Paul's admonition to *"let this mind be in you"* becomes the natural and inevitable outcome of the relationship.

It is a process that the devil does not want you to embark upon. Under no circumstances does he want you to receive the mind of Christ. You can be sure that the process of receiving the mind transplant is not and will not be pain-free!

Yet Christ suffered through it all, and as our example, He testifies that it is well worth the struggle. *"He shall see the labor of His soul, and be satisfied"* (Isa. 53:11).

Are you ready for the battle? Share your thoughts with the Lord and ask Him to provide you with the strength:

_____

_____

"When truth is working only upon the conscience, it creates much uneasiness; but when truth is invited into the heart, the whole being is brought into captivity to Jesus Christ. Even the thoughts are captured, for the mind of Christ works where the will is submitted to the will of God" (Mind, Character, and Personality, vol. 1, p. 324).

"The idea that Christian soldiers are to be excused from the conflicts, experiencing no trials, having all temporal comforts to enjoy, and even the luxuries of life, is a farce. The Christian conflict is a battle and a march, calling for endurance. Difficult work has to be done, and all who enlist as soldiers in Christ's army with these false ideas of pleasantness and ease, and then experience the trials, it often proves fatal to their Christianity. God does not present the reward to those whose whole life in this world has been one of self-indulgence and pleasure" (Manuscript Releases, vol. 14, pp. 27, 28).

Keep in mind that God created you for an eternity. Anything you give up or go through in this life will be rewarded in the next—and the blessings there will never cease!

➡ **Read Philippians 2:5-15.** Before you open His Word, ask the Lord to draw near to you. Consider the meaning of each verse and how it applies to your life. As you study Philippians . . .

✓ Realize that Jesus is your example in overcoming.

✓ Think about who He was in verse 6.

✓ Think about what He did and why He did it.

✓ Consider who He became and is today because of His choice to save you.

✓ Consider what He gave up for you.

✓ Realize what the Father did because Jesus acted as He did.

✓ Focus upon the fact that this is the mind you are to have.

✓ Notice that Jesus humbled Himself, surrendering His own will.

➡ **Write down** these 11 verses on notecards or paper so you can easily carry them with you. Use every opportunity to memorize these passages.

➡ **Tonight,** take time to pray and ask God to help you with your task. Each night, go through all 11 verses, even if you need to reread them.

➡ **Ask God** to give you the mind of Christ. Plead with Him to make it a reality in your life and trust that He will answer your prayer!

➡ **Remember,** this is an ongoing process, so continue this prayer regularly and believe that God will do for you what you ask of Him because it is His will.

➡ **Taking time with the Lord.** James 4:2 says, *"You do not have because you do not ask."* Tell God in prayer what you discovered about Jesus and yourself today and where you sense He is leading you. Ask Him for strength and purpose and guidance. He will provide these things because He wants you to succeed!

> *"I will give you a new heart and put a new spirit within you; I will take the heart of stone out of your flesh and give you a heart of flesh."*

The Master Worker

"O Lord, You are our Father; we are the clay,
and You our potter; and all we are the work of Your hand."
—Isaiah 64:8

The driving force of the Godhead is love. Love governs His every action. But before our creation, the devil slithered among the heavenly ranks and spread sophisticated lies about God. Unfortunately, humanity was not far behind many angels in believing "the father of lies."

Jesus came here to dispel those lies and revealed the Father's love in such a powerful way that the angels in heaven who still had some doubts were now fully convinced and reconciled to the Father (see Col. 1:20). This, however, has not stopped Satan. He continues with the same lie that he has been the one watching out for our best interests, not God!

I once had a nightmare that I will never forget. All of a sudden, I was standing on a mighty plain looking at a Celestial City in the distance when a giant of a man came up to me and said, "I resurrected you, and we can take that city!" A chill ran up my spine; it was the devil speaking! I did not want to be in the second resurrection. Instead, I want to go home with Jesus when He comes again!

How about you? Do you want to be in the first resurrection and stand with Jesus on the inside of the city—and not on the outside with Satan? _____

In order for that to happen, the Master Worker, with your permission, must mold and shape you. Your first vessel was ruined, so He needs to remake you. This reconstruction process is a necessity despite what Satan says.

> *"The word which came to Jeremiah from the Lord, saying: 'Arise and go down to the potter's house,
> and there I will cause you to hear My words.' Then I went down to the potter's house, and there he was,
> making something at the wheel. And the vessel that he made of clay was marred in the hand of the potter;
> so he made it again into another vessel, as it seemed good to the potter to make. Then the word of the Lord
> came to me, saying: 'O house of Israel, can I not do with you as this potter?' . . .
> 'Look, as the clay is in the potter's hand, so are you in My hand, O house of Israel!' "* (Jer. 18:1-6).

Will you give permission to the Master Worker to mold and remake you, even if there is some discomfort involved in the process? (Check all that apply.)

☐ I trust You, Lord.
☐ Yes, Father, remake me into Your image.
☐ Do whatever it takes to ensure I'm in the first resurrection with You.
☐ I don't want my stubbornness to cause me to end up on the outside of the city! Yes, work on me.
☐ The clay has no will of its own, so do as You will with me.
☐ Please, make me willing to be made willing.
☐ other: _____

The Process

"The potter takes the clay in his hands and molds and fashions it according to his own will. He kneads it and works it. He tears it apart and then presses it together. . . . Thus it becomes a vessel fit for use. So the great Master Worker desires to mold and fashion us. And as the clay is in the hands of the potter, so are we to be in His hands. We are not to try to do the work of the potter. Our part is to yield ourselves to the molding of the Master Worker" (*Testimonies for the Church*, vol. 8, pp. 186, 187).

Rewrite this statement in your own words and describe how it relates to your life:

_____

_____

_____

The Bible says, *"But now, O Lord, you are our Father; we are the clay, and You our potter; and all we are the work of Your hand"* (Isa. 64:8). In the following statement, **underline what you must do to be remade by the Master Worker:**

"The Potter cannot mold and fashion unto honor that which has never been placed in His hands. The Christian life is one of daily surrender, submission, and continual overcoming. Every day fresh victories will be gained. Self must be lost sight of, and the love of God must be constantly cultivated. Thus we grow up into Christ" (*Lift Him Up*, p. 65).

➡ **Ask the Master Worker** what transforming—reworking of the clay—needs to happen in you and listen to what He tells you. If He reveals something to you, list it below:

- _____

- _____

- _____

➡ **Now tell God that He has your permission to shape your life however He chooses.** But remember, this is an ongoing process—*do not* become discouraged if all the changes do not happen overnight!

"The Christian life is a life of warfare, of continual conflict. It is a battle and a march. But every act of obedience to Christ, every act of self-denial for His sake, every trial well endured, every victory gained over temptation, is a step in the march to the glory of final victory" (*Review and Herald*, Feb. 5, 1895).

➡ **Taking time with the Lord.** Ask your Father in heaven for His will to be combined with your will to create one omnipotent will. Say this prayer: "Heavenly Father, make me willing to be made willing." As you place yourself in God's gentle, caring hands, trust that you *are* making progress!

> *"O Lord, You are our Father; we are the clay, and You our potter; and all we are the work of Your hand."*

Unit 7, Day 5

Transformation in Action

"Not by works of righteousness which we have done,
but according to His mercy He saved us, through the washing
of regeneration and renewing of the Holy Spirit."
—Titus 3:5

"Christ is either Lord of all, or He is not Lord at all."
—Hudson Taylor

He was separated from his family in the devastating Somali conflict that tore his entire nation apart. As a young Muslim, Asha, not his real name, found himself in a refugee camp with several other young Muslims. While tuning the radio to their favorite program, they happened upon an Adventist World Radio (AWR) broadcast. Asha and his friends met Jesus Christ in those next few moments, and it changed their lives!

He fell so deeply in love with Jesus that he was determined to follow His Lord regardless of the personal cost. As divine destiny would have it, Asha was eventually able to leave Somalia and became the program producer for AWR's Somali-language broadcasts. Because of the danger involved in evangelizing in the Muslim nation, he produced his programs in secret for broadcast across all of Somalia from a distant location.

It is still not known how his whereabouts were revealed, but he was discovered by gun-toting thugs who hauled him to an undisclosed prison in Somalia. They attached electrical wires to his flesh and repeatedly hit the power. Over time, the torture caused him to lose much of his hearing and speech. Eventually, AWR was able to negotiate the release of this young Christian soldier and rushed him to a hospital in Nairobi, Kenya, where he regained his health.

We believed that once released from the hospital, Asha would never want to put himself in danger again. But nothing could have been further from the truth. Upon his release, Asha said, "It is the least I can do for my Lord." Today he is hiding in another country and still producing the life-changing programs that are reaching the Somali people for Christ.

➡ **Has this real-life account of service to God affected you—perhaps inspiring you to cling to your Lord more closely? If so, what will you do to feed that desire?**

_____

_____

"When souls are converted to God, they become mediums through which a vital current may be communicated for the transformation of the character of many others. Recovered themselves from Satan's power, they know how to work. Human nature becomes united with the divine nature, Christ lives in the human soul, and acts through all the powers of body, soul, and spirit. From the converted soul, light shines forth to those who are perishing. Those who have been in sin, and have experienced the love of Christ, know how to sympathize, how to adapt themselves to those who are in sin and sorrow, and can exercise the love of Christ through the channel of human affection" (Review and Herald, Nov. 12, 1895).

➡ **Read Acts 9:1-30,** then signify the correct answers below by circling true or false:

96

true / false: Saul experienced the rebirth process that began his transformation journey.

true / false: Everyone's rebirth experience is just as dramatic as Saul's.

true / false: Everyone must have a transformation experience.

true / false: Threats of killing Saul could not stop him from sharing Jesus.

true / false: The power to witness under the threat of death comes from my own strength.

true / false: Jesus said that Saul (later called Paul) was to suffer for Him.

true / false: Christians do not need to suffer for the gospel's sake.

true / false: By His grace I will follow my Lord and go and do whatever He asks.

true / false: Some things are just too hard for the Lord to accomplish in me.

true / false: All of His biddings are enablings.

➡ **Read Mark 14:29-31** and then answer the questions below.

Under what power was Peter and the other disciples functioning at that time?

_____

It is evident that they tried to stand for God in their own strength. What were the results?

_____

You might never be called upon to be a Christian martyr, but the perils you will face are great just the same. It's true for every child of the King. The keys to overcoming are to be willing to face them and to acknowledge that only God's grace and power can see you through.

➡ **In the following text, underline the action on Peter's part that later led him to deny His Lord.**

> *"Those who had laid hold of Jesus led Him away to Caiaphas the high priest,*
> *where the scribes and the elders were assembled. But Peter followed*
> *Him at a distance to the high priest's courtyard.*
> *And he went in and sat with the servants to see the end"* (Matt. 26:57, 58).

If you follow Christ from a distance in a spiritual sense, you will give the devil enough room to step in between you—just as he did with Peter.

"Satan knows your weakness; therefore cling to Jesus. Abiding in God's love, you may stand every test. The righteousness of Christ alone can give you power to stem the tide of evil that is sweeping over the world. Bring faith into your experience. Faith lightens every burden, relieves every weariness. Providences that are now mysterious you may solve by continued trust in God. Walk by faith in the path He marks out. Trials will come, but go forward. This will strengthen your faith and fit you for service. The records of sacred history are written, not merely that we may read and wonder, but that the same faith which wrought in God's servants of old may work in us. In no less marked manner will the Lord work now, wherever there are hearts of faith to be channels of His power" (Prophets and Kings, p. 175).

➡ **Taking time with the Lord.** Pray that there will be no distance between you and God!

> *"Not by works of righteousness which we have done,*
> *but according to his mercy he saved us, through the washing*
> *of regeneration and renewing of the Holy Spirit."*

8

Are You Tempted?

Ron Hutchcraft in his book *Wake Up Calls* shares this moment in art history that says a lot about the human condition:

> "In 1982 *ABC Evening News* reported on an unusual work of modern art—a chair affixed to a shotgun. It was to be viewed by sitting in the chair and looking directly into the gun barrel. The gun was loaded and set on a timer to fire at an undetermined moment within the next hundred years. The amazing thing was that people waited in lines to sit and stare into the shell's path! They all knew the gun could go off at point-blank range at any moment, but they were gambling that the fatal blast wouldn't happen during their minute in the chair. Yes, it was foolhardy, yet many people who wouldn't dream of sitting in that chair live a lifetime gambling that they can get away with sin. Foolishly they ignore the risk until the inevitable self-destruction."

There is nothing that can force you to sit down in the chair of temptation and wait for the devil to pull the trigger. Rather, we need to keep choosing to stand upon holy ground—God's ground—and ignore the devil.

"For the death that He died, He died to sin once for all; but the life that He lives, He lives to God. Likewise you also, reckon yourselves to be dead indeed to sin, but alive to God in Christ Jesus our Lord. Therefore do not let sin reign in your mortal body, that you should obey it in its lusts. And do not present your members as instruments of unrighteousness to sin, but present yourselves to God as being alive from the dead, and your members as instruments of righteousness to God" (Rom. 6:10-13).

Our study for this week will be about understanding the nature of temptation and how to avoid falling into the devil's traps.

Biblical Truth!

"No temptation has overtaken you except such as is common to man;
but God is faithful, who will not allow you to be tempted
beyond what you are able, but with the temptation will also make the way
of escape, that you may be able to bear it."
—1 Corinthians 10:13

Growing up in a country setting, I went fishing from a very early age. As soon as I was old enough, my dad placed a fishing pole in my hands and taught me the fine art of temptation. What do I mean? Allow me to show you by sharing several synonyms of the word "temptation"—lure, attraction, pull, seduction, inducement, etc.

I was taught to place the finest worms on the hook in the most appealing way and to then caress the water at the precise location, allowing the worms to gently float past the prime resting spot of the "big one." This was all done to tempt the fish in the most irresistible way possible, and most of the time, the inevitable would happen—a fish in my frying pan!

Describe in your own words the term *temptation*:

_____

_____

➡ **Circle true or false for each statement below:**

true / false: I am doomed to accept temptation and sin as a fact of life.

true / false: Eve had to accept the temptation of Satan in the garden.

true / false: The devil tries to lure, attract, pull, and seduce me into sin.

true / false: The devil tried to tempt Jesus but was unsuccessful.

true / false: Satan does not mind if I serve God with all of my heart.

true / false: The devil is my adversary and not my friend.

true / false: I do not need to "bite" on the temptations of the devil.

➡ **Read Mark 1:13 and 1 Peter 5:8.**

I'm convinced that the devil desperately doesn't want you to believe that temptation is not sin itself or that God has the power to keep you from surrendering to it.

It is a total lie that you must accept as biblical fact that falling for any temptation is unavoidable. You and I have been held captive to this lie for far too long! Hebrews 4:15 says, *"When [Jesus] lived on earth, he was tempted in every way that we are, but he did not sin"* (ICB). Amazing!

Jesus was our example, and if He was able to avoid temptation then you and I are well able to avoid temptation too! There is no pressure to sin that is greater than the power of the Almighty to deliver you from it.

Do you understand that temptation is not sin? _____

➡ **Fill in the missing words and phrases:**

"And do not lead us into _____, but deliver us from the evil one. For Yours is the kingdom and the power" (Matt. 6:13).

"No temptation has overtaken you except such as is common to man; but God is faithful, who will not allow you to be ___ _____, but with the temptation will also make _____, that you may be able to bear it" (1 Cor. 10:13).

An Amazing Promise

*"Those who are partakers of the divine nature **will not give way to temptation.** The enemy is working with all his might to overcome those who are striving to live the Christian life. He comes to them with temptations, in the hope that they will yield. Thus he hopes to discourage them. But those who have planted their feet firmly on the Rock of Ages **will not yield** to his devices. They will remember that God is their Father and Christ their Helper. The Savior came to our world to bring to every tried, tempted soul strength to **overcome even as He overcame.** I know the power of temptation; I know the dangers that are in the way; but I know, too, that strength sufficient for every time of need is provided for those who are struggling against temptation"* (Messages to Young People, p. 81; emphasis supplied).

How does this promise make you feel? Will it help you to focus upon the Lord and the help He offers?

_____

➡ **Fill in the missing words or phrases:**

"Therefore submit to God. _____ the devil and he will _____" (James 4:7).

"The Lord knows how to deliver the godly _____" (2 Peter 2:9).

"Do not _____ your members as instruments of unrighteousness to sin, but _____ to God as being alive from the dead, and your members as instruments of righteousness to God. For sin _____ _____ over you" (Rom. 6:13, 14).

Here's a message full of hope that you need to take to heart: *"Through belief in Satan's misrepresentation of God, man's character and destiny were changed, but if men will believe in the Word of God, they will be transformed in mind and character, and fitted for eternal life"* (Selected Messages, book 1, p. 346).

➡ **Fill in the missing words or phrases:**

"Yet in all these things we _____ through Him who loved us. For I am persuaded that neither death nor life, nor angels nor principalities nor powers . . . nor any other created thing, shall be able to _____ _____" (Rom. 8:37-39).

"Your word I have hidden in my heart, that I might _____ against You" (Ps. 119:11).

William Butler Yeats once wrote, "Every conquered temptation represents a new fund of moral energy. Every trial endured and weathered in the right spirit makes a soul nobler and stronger than it was before." Amen!

"Christ is a conqueror, and those who follow him will be on the conquering side. There are precious victories before the Christian. He may be weak, but the Redeemer knows his need, and is able to strengthen him. Jesus knows that Satan is trying to get control of men and women, and He stands ready to help all who come to Him for help. He is not willing that any should perish. He has made it possible for every tempted son and daughter of Adam, in every time of temptation, to gain a glorious victory. He has placed the power of heaven within the reach of His children" (Youth's Instructor, Oct. 3, 1901).

➡ **Taking time with the Lord.** In prayer, thank God that you are not deceived by the lies of the evil one. Thank your Lord that He has gained the victory over sin so, in Him and by His power, you will too.

> *"No temptation has overtaken you except such as is common to man; but God is faithful, who will not allow you to be tempted beyond what you are able, but with the temptation will also make the way of escape, that you may be able to bear it."*

The First Look

"Submit to God. Resist the devil and he will flee from you."
—James 4:7

"What makes resisting temptation difficult for many people
is that they don't want to discourage it completely."
—Benjamin Franklin

➡ **Read the account of Eve's temptation in Genesis 3:1-13.**

What was the result of her temptation?

_____

"Adam and Eve were placed on trial and failed. . . . Satan deceived Eve, and she disobeyed God. The holy pair, not resisting temptation, were brought under Satan's jurisdiction. The enemy gained supremacy over the human race, bringing in death, the penalty of disobedience" (Christ Triumphant, p. 289).

How should we deal with temptations, especially those that seem overwhelming at the time?

_____

_____

➡ **Read the story of Joseph's temptation in Genesis 39:1-23.** Check all that apply:

☐ The devil used Potiphar's wife as bait to try to hook Joseph.

☐ Joseph should not have entered the house without someone else going in also.

☐ Joseph said he would not sin against Potiphar.

☐ He should have had some fun; he would not have ended up in prison.

☐ I would have done things differently had I been Joseph. Explain:

_____

_____

Because Joseph was a slave, he couldn't just leave his job—but could he have done anything else to avoid the temptation? Explain:

_____

Chomping down on the lure of temptation denies God His opportunity to work in our lives, so Joseph refused to sin against God. Will you also allow God to work in you to overcome and let temptations pass on downstream? _____

"There is no safety for any man . . . unless he feels the necessity of seeking God for counsel at every step. Those only who maintain close communion with God will learn to place His estimate upon men, to reverence the pure, the good, the humble, and the meek. The heart must be garrisoned as was that of Joseph. Then temptations to depart from integrity will be met with decision: 'How then can I do this great wickedness, and sin against God?' The strongest temptation is no excuse for sin. . . . Sin is your own act. The seat of the difficulty is the unrenewed heart" (The Adventist Home, p. 331).

Is there any excuse whatsoever for you to accept the devil's temptation to sin? _____

When Eve found herself looking at the tree of the knowledge of good and evil, she should have turned away immediately and fled the scene. Her downfall was the second look!

> *"Eve was beguiled by the serpent and made to believe that God would not do as He had said. She ate, and, thinking she felt the sensation of a new and more exalted life, she bore the fruit to her husband. The serpent had said that she should not die, and she felt no ill effects from eating the fruit, nothing which could be interpreted to mean death, but, instead, a pleasurable sensation, which she imagined was as the angels felt. Her experience stood arrayed against the positive command of Jehovah"* (Counsels on Health, p. 108).

Have you ever hung around for the second look? _____ . How did it turn out for you?

_____

_____

Have you noticed, as did Eve, that the pleasure of the sin lasts only for a short while? _____

Here is the problem with taking more than one look. (The first look notifies you that it is a temptation.) When you take the second look, you're participating in reverse-transformation:

> *"By beholding we become changed. Though formed in the image of his Maker, man can so educate his mind that sin which he once loathed will become pleasant to him. As he ceases to watch and pray, he ceases to guard the citadel, the heart, and engages in sin and crime. The mind is debased, and it is impossible to elevate it from corruption while it is being educated to enslave the moral and intellectual powers and bring them in subjection to grosser passions. Constant war against the carnal mind must be maintained; and we must be aided by the refining influence of the grace of God, which will attract the mind upward and habituate it to meditate upon pure and holy things"* (The Adventist Home, p. 330).

➡ **In the preceding paragraph,** underline what happens when you take a second look at temptation. Then circle those things you can do, through God's power, to help turn the situation around.

The following quotes offer some great insight into the typical human experience when dealing with temptation:

> *"Most people would like to be delivered from temptation but would like it to keep in touch."*—Robert Orben.

> *"Temptation usually comes in through a door that has been deliberately left open."*—Arnold Glasow.

Do you resolve to surrender all to God and no longer remain in touch with temptation? Explain:

_____

_____

Have you left open any doors in your life that will allow temptation to come in unhindered? And if you have, what do you choose to do about it now?

_____

_____

➡ **Taking time with the Lord.** Say this prayer: "Father, I have been born into sin, but You have provided the way out! You have gained the victory over every single temptation the devil set in front of You. You looked only long enough to recognize them as temptations and then You immediately turned away. Please help me to do the same. I need Your power—Your Spirit. As I rely on You, give me the same victories. Enable me to recognize temptation and to turn away. Thank You for your amazing love for me. I need You every moment of every day. Thank You that You have beaten the devil for me and will answer this prayer. In Jesus' name, amen."

Avoiding Temptation

"Lead me, O Lord, in Your righteousness because of my enemies;
make Your way straight before my face."
—Psalm 5:8

"God is better served in resisting a temptation to evil than in many formal prayers."
—William Penn

Even better than resisting temptation when confronted with it is to do all you can to avoid it in the first place. For instance, if you were an alcoholic, you wouldn't choose to hang out in a bar. If you were addicted to porn, you would limit your Internet access.

➡ **Read Hebrews 11:24-26**.

The difference between those who fall and those who overcome is how they respond to temptation. Moses began to realize that his earthly power and massive riches could become a snare to him. His career track as a prince of Egypt was not worth the potential loss of eternal salvation. He therefore avoided the temptation by surrendering his own will to the will of God, thereby choosing the better reward.

The best choice always is to avoid every temptation to begin with, as Moses did, and separate from it. Are there avoidable temptations still waiting for you in your home, your office, your recreation time, or elsewhere? If so, list them here:

_____

Is flirting with these potential temptations really worth more than eternal life and happiness? **After identifying areas of potential temptations in your life, how can you adjust your life to avoid them?**

_____

_____

God desires you to have a radical Christian experience, and it might mean a major shift in your priorities. If you were in line to become president of the United States but realized it could cause you to lose your relationship with the Lord, would you give it up?

➡ **Read the account of the life of Judas in the passage below.** As the treasurer for the disciples, he had the most amazing opportunities to walk with God, but the lure of silver finally became too much for him.

"When Judas first united with the twelve, he manifested a spirit subordinate to his Master. He loved the great Teacher. . . . There came to him a desire to be changed in spirit and inclination, and he hoped to experience this by connecting himself with Christ. Yes; in the companionship of Christ, Judas might have found continual strength and aid; he might have cooperated with Christ in overcoming temptation, instead of yielding to the suggestions of Satan.

"Knowing that he was being corrupted by covetousness, Christ gave him the privilege of hearing many precious lessons. He heard Christ laying down the principles which all must possess who would enter his kingdom. He was given every opportunity to receive Christ as his personal Savior, but he refused this gift. He would not yield his way and will to

Christ. He did not practice that which was contrary to his own inclinations; therefore his strong avaricious spirit was not corrected. While he continued a disciple in outward form, and while in the very presence of Christ, he appropriated to himself means that belonged to the Lord's treasury" (*Review and Herald*, Oct. 5, 1897).

➡ **Write a short synopsis** of Judas' life in your own words, knowing that the end for Judas came when he went out and hanged himself because he betrayed his Lord for 30 pieces of silver.

_____

_____

_____

Judas had needed to put into practice the things taught by Jesus—and total surrender was at the top of the list. Review the following promise of God written down by Ellen White: *"As the will of man cooperates with the will of God, it becomes omnipotent"* (*Christ's Object Lessons*, p. 333).

Does this really mean you can turn away and avoid falling into temptation? _____

It's exactly what it means! Now, as best you can, use the following words and phrases to fill in the blanks in the statement below:

in	denying	any cost	follow
from	take up	leave	obeying

"Jesus died, not to save man _____ his sins, but _____ his sins. Man is to _____ the error of his ways, to _____ the example of Christ, to _____ his cross and follow Him, _____ self, and _____ God at _____" (*Testimonies for the Church*, vol. 4, p. 251).*

Victory is all about understanding the correct use of the human will. Do you see the pattern? It is no accident that the words "leave," "follow," "denying," "obeying," and "at any cost"—in that order—are connected with overcoming in Christ.

➡ **Read Matthew 7:21.**

What is the will of the Father?

_____

Check all that apply:

☐ By God's power, I will avoid temptation when I see the potential arise.
☐ I am learning to flee to Jesus when I recognize temptations.
☐ I am reprioritizing my life to become all God wants me to become.
☐ I am walking closer with God each day.
☐ I am struggling, but He is good to me and will help me.
☐ I choose to behold Him more each day.
☐ I am experiencing His amazing power in my life.
☐ I can see that my life is changing—for the better.
☐ other: _____

➡ **Taking time with the Lord.** Say this prayer: "Father, lead me not into temptation, but deliver me from evil."

_____

*Answers in order: in, from, leave, follow, take up, denying, obeying, any cost.

The Devil Made Me Do It

"We ourselves were also once foolish, disobedient, deceived,
serving various lusts and pleasures, living in malice and envy,
hateful and hating one another."
—Titus 3:3

"No mortal man or devil can supersede the plan of God for your life.
If you lay hold of this truth, it will set you free. But there is only one person
who can get you out of the will of God and that person is you."
—John Bevere

The comedian Flip Wilson was famous for his one-liner "The devil made me do it!" Across America and the world, every stupid or sinful thing people do is followed by some variation of "the devil made me do it."

Oscar Wilde once said, "I can resist everything except temptation." Mae West added, "I generally avoid temptation unless I can't resist it." And I must confess that before God woke me up to His reality, I used Wilson's line with regularity, and I have even laughed at Wilde's and West's statements, too. But a saying that brings all this into perspective is that of William Shakespeare: "Temptation is the fire that brings up the scum of the heart."

Wow! Does that nail it or what? "Scum" describes the filth oozing from the heart of the one who is overcome by the devil's temptations. But understand that the devil *cannot make* you do anything you choose not to do. This truth must become central to your Christian experience!

➡ **Below, circle the things God is asking you to do:**

> "Gird up the loins of your mind, be sober, and rest your hope fully upon the grace
> that is to be brought to you at the revelation of Jesus Christ; as obedient children,
> not conforming yourselves to the former lusts, as in your ignorance; but as He who called you is holy,
> you also be holy in all your conduct, because it is written, 'Be holy, for I am holy'" (1 Peter 1:13-16).

I had been working in Bangladesh for a time when the mission president gave me the very nice gift of a lungi. It is the traditional dress for men there, consisting of a long and wide sewn piece of cloth forming a tube. He placed it on me and showed me how to tie it. Then, standing behind me and reaching between my legs, he grabbed a handful of cloth and said, "Now I'm going to show you how to gird yourself according to the Bible." With a swift yank he jerked the lungi cloth up between my legs so hard that he lifted me off the ground! Then he tucked it in to my waist area. In an instant I was girded! Grinning from ear to ear, he said, "Now you are ready for battle!"

I will never forget that lesson! It's the same counsel Peter is giving when he says to *"gird up the loins of your mind."* He is saying, "Prepare for battle with the devil."

➡ **Read over the following counsel carefully and pray:**

> "Gird up the loins of your mind, says the apostle; then control your thoughts, not allowing them to have full scope. The

thoughts may be guarded and controlled by your own determined efforts. Think right thoughts, and you will perform right actions. You have, then, to guard the affections, not letting them go out and fasten upon improper objects. Jesus has purchased you with His own life; you belong to Him; therefore He is to be consulted in all things, as to how the powers of your mind and the affections of your heart shall be employed" (*The Adventist Home*, p. 54).

From this statement, list the things you are counseled to do:

- _____
- _____
- _____
- _____
- _____

Are you working, through the power of God's Spirit, on doing some or all of these things? In the list above, underline the items you are working on now and circle the ones you have not started yet.

➡ **Read James 1:12-16.**

Every sin has its roots anchored in these three areas of temptations. Raise your antenna and always be on guard for the . . .

Lust of the flesh:
Food, drugs, and alcohol fit into this category, along with many other consumable items. It is evident in our world that this is a major area of temptation. It was part of the temptation that hooked Eve. Abuse of the natural appetite was also the first temptation the devil tried to hook Jesus with when he said, *"Turn these stones to bread."*

Lust of the eyes:
After Eve fell, she ran to Adam as the devil's tempter. Adam saw what she had done and knew that the penalty for her disobedience was death. He looked upon her beauty and decided he desired the woman more than he desired God, so he took the fruit and ate.

Pride of life:
So many things fit into this category—but we'll focus on power, fame, and wealth. None of these things are sins in and of themselves, but power, fame, and wealth are easily abused by those who aren't humble before God, and they can become idols to those who seek after them before they seek after God. Satan tempted Eve with power she was not meant to have, and her pride of life won out over her love for God.

Based on today's study, circle true or false below:

true / false: The devil cannot make me accept any temptation, no matter how alluring!

true / false: Jesus is my example. He depended on the Father's power and never sinned.

true / false: Jesus will live in me and give me the same power to resist all temptation.

true / false: There are things I must overcome in my life.

true / false: Jesus knows I am too weak to avoid temptation.

In *The Screwtape Letters* C. S. Lewis wrote, "The safest road to Hell is the gradual one—the gentle slope, soft underfoot, without sudden turnings, without milestones, without signposts."

"Because you have kept My command to persevere, I also will keep you from the hour of trial which shall come upon the whole world, to test those who dwell on the earth" (Rev. 3:10).

➡ **Taking time with the Lord.** Is there anything you sense that God wants to say to you at this time? Write it down and spend time talking to Him about it in prayer.

_____

_____

_____

_____

{ *"We ourselves were also once foolish, disobedient, deceived, serving various lusts and pleasures, living in malice and envy, hateful and hating one another."* }

His Biddings

"May the God of all grace, who called us to His eternal glory by Christ Jesus,
after you have suffered a while, perfect, establish, strengthen, and settle you."
—1 Peter 5:10

"We are too busy to pray, and so we are too busy to have power. We have a great
deal of activity, but we accomplish little; many services but few conversions;
much machinery but few results."
—R. A. Torrey

As we begin today's study, I invite you to seek God in prayer, asking Him to be with you in a special way and providing you with the power to become all He bids you to become.

➡ **Read Matthew 14:28-31.**

At Jesus' bidding, and as the other 11 disciples sat spellbound, Peter faithfully stepped out onto the violent waves smashing against the boat. He began walking on water—but something went wrong. Share the reason you believe Jesus told Peter that he had so little faith:

_____

The Greek wording indicates that the question to Peter was really *"Why do you have so little confidence in Me?"* It was a good question; after all, Jesus was the one who first called Peter out of the boat. But in the middle of the exercise Peter lost sight of Christ and sank.

How do you think Peter and Jesus got back to the boat?

_____

Scripture doesn't really tell us how they got back to the boat, but I have a strong feeling that they walked together on the water—not swam—back. Why? Because . . .

> *"Whatever is to be done at His command may be accomplished in His strength. All His biddings are enablings"* (*Christ's Object Lessons*, p. 333).

Once Jesus beckoned Peter to come to Him, He was not going to let the disciple down. Jesus bade Peter to walk on top of the water—not in it! The question is Would you have gotten out of the boat at the command of Jesus and walked on the water? _____

Has God asked you to "go" or "do" for Him and you refused?

_____

Do you believe that all His biddings are enablings, regardless of what He asks you to do?
- ☐ No.
- ☐ Yes.
- ☐ I'm not sure.

➡ **Read Joshua 3:15-17.** It's another story that involves a lot of water, but this time God said to get into the water.

The Lord instructed the priests to take the ark and walk into the Jordon River during its flood stage. As soon as they did, the waters ceased from flowing until the people, perhaps a million or more, passed through the riverbed.

If you had been one of those priests, what would you have been thinking as you walked toward a flooding river knowing that the ark weighed so much your feet would stay glued to the bottom? Try to put yourself in their sandals. Yet Jesus teaches us that it doesn't matter if it's on top of the waves or under them—*"all His biddings are enablings."*

Do you believe Jesus? Explain why or why not:

_____

_____

The Pharisees brought to Jesus a woman caught in adultery. They believed they had laid a clever trap for Him, but Jesus beat them at their own game. He then turned all of His attention to the woman, who just knew she was going to be stoned to death. He asked her if there was anyone to condemn her. *"She said, 'No one, Lord.' And Jesus said to her, 'Neither do I condemn you; **go and sin no more**'"* (John 8:11).

➡ **Fill in the blanks:**

"All His _____ are _____."

Jesus came upon a paralytic at the Pool of Bethesda and healed him. The man ran to the Temple praising God. Afterward, Jesus found the man at the Temple and said to him, *"See, you have been made well. **Sin no more,** lest a worse thing come upon you"* (John 5:14).

Do you see it plainly? Jesus is bidding us, you and me, to *"sin no more."* Will you follow His command? What is harder—to walk on water or to sin no more? Why? _____

_____

_____

Do you believe the power of God is just a side benefit for the Christian, to be used only whenever you decide? Or is it explosive power and authority emanating from the indwelling Spirit, which will actively separate you from the clutches of the devil and transform you into God's image? Which is it? It is your choice. _____

_____

_____

➡ **Read John 1:12. Whom does God give power to?**

_____

Here is a practical example of how this power and process have been working in my own life. (Remember, transformation is a process.)

After shopping at the grocery story, I make my way to the checkout stand, where, invariably, a long line of people stand in my way. The waiting begins. The counter space near these checkout lines is referred to as the "impulse section." Customers are enticed to grab the items as a last-second impulse.

The only things to really look at while you're standing there are the candy, gum, and magazines. The gum and candy can hold my attention for only so long, so my attention sometimes moves to the magazines. What usually adorns the covers of such magazines as *People, Us, Vogue,* and others? That's right—beautiful women with few clothes on. It's impulse shopping at its worst for men.

Now in those moments I have two choices. Option one, I like what I see and keep looking, or two, I recognize it's the devil's bait, refuse to keep looking, and pray for strength to honor God and resist feeding the lust of the eyes.

I choose option two and turn away, but I am enabled to do so only by the power of Christ's mind—the mind I acquired that morning because I spent time with Him in Bible study and prayer. I chose to die to self, acknowledging to God that His choices for me should also be my choices for myself.

Remember, *"all His biddings are enablings,"* and He bids us to separate from sin. His power enables us to do so!

Is God asking you to separate from something? Will you choose to do so now? Write down your answer:

_____

_____

One problem destroying the lives of many people in the church and in the world is Internet pornography. No one is immune. I have a friend whose life and that of his entire family have recently been destroyed over this "company" that comes to visit in the privacy of his home. This scum that attempts to rise up in the human heart seeks to destroy all who are curious. This is a life-or-death matter, and you must be continually on guard! Cling to Jesus and His power if this temptation is affecting you and your family.

> *"The company we choose will be a help or a hindrance to us. We are not to run any risk by placing ourselves where evil angels will surround us with their temptations and their snares. Satan . . . puts his alluring temptations before the soul. He appears as an angel of light and clothes his temptations with apparent goodness. Our first work is to disentangle ourselves from everything that is in any way calculated to tarnish the soul"* (In Heavenly Places, p. 170).

Remember that behind every enticing photo and video, a demon with bared fangs—dripping with the blood of his last victim—is waiting to destroy you!

You can overcome this sin and every other sin in the same way Jesus did:

> *"It was from the Father that Christ constantly drew the power that enabled Him to keep His life free from spot or stain of sin. It was this power that enabled Him to resist temptation"* (Review and Herald, July 4, 1912).

What a wonderful promise! When temptations come knocking, send Jesus to the door. This power and help are yours for the asking. Yes, you are destined to become transformed into the image of Jesus Christ!

➡ **Write your name in the blank space below:**

> *"As the will of _____ cooperates with the will of God, it becomes omnipotent. Whatever is to be done at His command may be accomplished in His strength. All His biddings are enablings."*

➡ **Taking time with the Lord.** Ask God for His power to flood your life and purge you from any and all evil and sin, to lift you up higher and still higher above the scum of this earth. He will enable you to overcome *all* sin in your life . . . *every* temptation! If you will choose to get out of the boat, He will walk with you on top of the waves—you will become a water walker! Thank Him for the power and especially for His amazing love to you regardless of your past.

> *"May the God of all grace, who called us to His eternal glory by Christ Jesus, after you have suffered a while, perfect, establish, strengthen, and settle you."*

9

Becoming Fireproof

On that great day when Jesus returns to our planet, many will discover too late that all sin is combustible. At His approach the cleansing fire will become unbearable, and they will scramble for a hiding place.

"The kings of the earth, the great men, the rich men . . . every slave and every free man, hid themselves in the caves and in the rocks of the mountains, and said to the mountains and rocks, 'Fall on us and hide us from the face of Him who sits on the throne and from the wrath of the Lamb! For the great day of His wrath has come, and who is able to stand?'" (Rev. 6:15-17).

This is a good question. Who is going to be ready to stand on the day when the Great Judge comes with millions of angels? Those who have been preparing for eternity prior to this event, those who have allowed God to separate them from all combustibles—sin.

"The heavens and the earth . . . are reserved for fire until the day of judgment and perdition of ungodly men" (2 Peter 3:7).

Yes, unlike those who will be scrambling for the rocks to hide themselves, there will be those who have been waiting in great expectation for His return:

"It will be said in that day: 'Behold, this is our God; we have waited for Him, and He will save us. This is the Lord; we have waited for Him; we will be glad and rejoice in His salvation'" (Isa. 25:9).

So the question is . . .

"Since all these things will be dissolved, what manner of persons ought you to be in holy conduct and godliness?" (2 Peter 3:11).

Isn't it time to make sure that God is given permission to burn out *every sin* in your life? This can be accomplished only by falling more deeply in love with Him, allowing Him to occupy every corner of your heart so that nothing else can—hence, you become fireproof!

Highlighting Your Bible

"I will look to the Lord; I will wait for the God of my salvation;
my God will hear me."
—Micah 7:7

"The Bible was not given for our information but for our transformation."
—Dwight L. Moody

During my ongoing journey of becoming a closer friend to Christ, He led me to start highlighting my Bible. I was actually staying in Guatemala with a friend, and we were overlooking a pretty jungle river. It was a very relaxing time. In that moment God impressed me to start reading my Bible with a yellow highlighter in hand.

I started to mark every text that spoke of:

1. The power of God and His desire to share that power with us
2. The desire of God to separate us from sin
3. The happiness found when we separate from sin
4. The need to become overcomers in this life
5. God's desire to abide with us to enable us to become like Him.

The numerous highlights revealed an unmistakable, overwhelming lesson! God longs to give us total victory over sin, separate us from the devil, and keep us from temptation.

- **Find a yellow highlighter and begin your own Bible-marking process,** starting in 1 John 1-5. Use my five points above as a reference for marking. If the Lord impresses you to mark other areas germane to transformation, by all means do so.

- **Taking time with the Lord.** Prayerfully consider whether God has led you to any new spiritual discoveries today. List them—use extra paper as necessary:

_____

_____

_____

_____

"I will look to the Lord; I will wait for the God of my salvation; my God will hear me."

Living in the Spirit

"Clearly you are an epistle of Christ, ministered by us,
written not with ink but by the Spirit of the living God,
not on tablets of stone but on tablets of flesh, that is, of the heart."
—2 Corinthians 3:3

"You will keep him in perfect peace, whose mind is stayed on You,
because he trusts in You. Trust in the Lord forever, for . . .
the Lord is everlasting strength."
—Isaiah 26:3, 4

➡ **Prayerfully read Romans 6:1 to Romans 8:18.** You might even want to use your highlighter as you go along!

In Romans 1 to 5 Paul set forth God's free gift of justification, but in Romans 6 through 8 he sets out the path to godliness—the way of living in the Holy Spirit and the Holy Sprit living in us. You are daily learning to walk closer and closer with your God. Those who experience the transformation process will demonstrate it in their daily lives.

Have a blessed day as you walk with your Lord and listen to Him speak to you through the pages of His Living Word!

➡ **Taking time with the Lord.** You encountered God today as you listened to Him speaking to you through His Word. Prayerfully consider what He shared with you and write it down below.

_____

_____

_____

_____

"Clearly you are an epistle of Christ, ministered by us, written not with ink but by the Spirit of the living God, not on tablets of stone but on tablets of flesh, that is, of the heart."

Of Pearls and Hidden Treasure

"Those who will search the Scriptures for themselves, because it is the Word of God, who are willing to dig for the truth as for hidden treasures, will receive for their prize that wisdom which cometh from God. If they will not rely upon their own smartness, and not trust in their own inventions and their supposed fruitful minds, if they will give the working of the mind into the Lord's hands, and yoke up with Jesus Christ, they will not take steps where Jesus does not lead the way."
—Ellen G. White*

I once met an older man, Mila, in a tiny village in the mountains of Nepal, an incredibly harsh region in which to live.

He shared with me that he had been a Buddhist monk for most of his life but had never experienced any real peace in his life. That might sound strange coming from a Buddhist, but it's not when you realize there is only One who can bring true peace to every person.

Mila guided me through the mountains to what had been his temple. It was beautiful! Moreover, brightly clothed monks were everywhere, and, as it happened, I was there during their special services. The massive sounds of their horns echoed throughout the golden pillars, and the clear "ting" of the cymbals raised my expectation of the event. The sweet-smelling incense wafted upward to mingle with the sounds of syncopated chants.

Human senses might be able to absorb the wonderfulness of the service, but Mila could find no peace in this ancient religion, nor did he find it in the beautiful temple. But one day, as he was tuning his old tube radio to the BBC News station, he stumbled across the Adventist World Radio's *Peace and Happiness* program. He told me, "I heard them talk of Jesus, and, for the first time in my life, I experienced peace. Now I save my money all week long so I can take the bus to church, because it is very far away. All the neighbors say that those people pay me to go to church, but I tell them, 'No, it is because I love Jesus!'"

Mila gave up everything in his life for real treasure. How about you—is the happiness and peace that comes only from Jesus worth everything to you? _____

➡ **Read Matthew 13:44-46.** Jesus tells two parables here. Circle the required response in order to obtain the treasure.

"The kingdom of heaven is like treasure hidden in a field, which a man found and hid; and for joy over it he goes and sells all that he has and buys that field" (verse 44).

"The kingdom of heaven is like a merchant seeking beautiful pearls, who, when he had found one pearl of great price, . . . sold all that he had and bought it" (verses 45, 46).

According to Jesus, how much did each person give to obtain the treasure or the pearl of great price? _____

"In the parable the pearl is not represented as a gift. The merchantman bought it at the price of all that he had. Many question the meaning of this, since Christ is represented in the Scriptures as a gift. He is a gift, but only to those who give themselves, soul, body, and spirit, to Him without reserve. We are to give ourselves to Christ, to live a life of willing obedience to all His requirements. All that we are, all the talents and capabilities we possess, are the

Lord's, to be consecrated to His service. When we thus give ourselves wholly to Him, Christ, with all the treasures of heaven, gives Himself to us. We obtain the pearl of great price" (*Christ's Object Lessons*, p. 116).

Christ and heaven are worth all that we are and possess. Is there any part of your life that is worth too much—too precious to you—to give up in order to obtain heaven?

_____

➡ **Read Matthew 21:28-31.** Describe who is going to enter the kingdom and why:

_____

_____

_____

_____

Jesus is calling you to be His servant. The servant never debates the orders of the master, but simply obeys. According to the parable, it matters not what your past has been; it's only what you do in the present that counts.

After 65 years Mila's focus turned from himself to Jesus—that's when his real life began. As the hymn goes: "Turn your eyes upon Jesus, . . . and the things of earth will grow strangely dim, in the light of His glory and grace." Will you serve Jesus today by giving Him 100 percent?

The Bible says, *"You will show me the path of life; in Your presence is fullness of joy; at Your right hand are pleasures forevermore"* (Ps. 16:11). Are you ready to sell all you have in order to obtain the treasure of infinite worth? _____

_____

The apostle Paul gave 100 percent to Christ. He had his priorities straight:

> *"At one time all these things were important to me. But now I think those things are worth nothing because of Christ. Not only those things, but I think that all things are worth nothing compared with the greatness of knowing Christ Jesus my Lord. Because of Christ, I have lost all those things. And now I know that all those things are worthless trash. . . . Now that I belong to Christ, I am right with God. . . . All I want is to know Christ"* (Phil. 3:7-10, ICB).

➡ **A Prayer of Submission and Commitment:** If you are ready in your heart, humbly come before the Lord at this time and share the following with Him. Don't rush through the list, but pause after each request and listen to the Lord:

1. Bring me into a wholehearted love relationship with You.
2. Help me to become Your friend.
3. Help me to hear Your voice, as the sheep hears the shepherd's voice.
4. I choose to be Your child with no restrictions whatsoever!
5. I lay everything I am and all I own at Your feet to do with as You wish, because I want nothing to come between us.
6. Bless me with an abundant measure of Your Holy Spirit every day.
7. Guide me at every step on my transformation journey.
8. I give You permission to do whatever it takes to get me to heaven.
9. Father, always make me willing to be made willing.
10. other: _____

Check the appropriate box regarding the prayer above:
☐ I am not completely ready to commit my life to God, so I did not pray this prayer.
☐ I am committed to following God at any and all costs, so I prayed this prayer.

If you are not ready to fully commit your life to the Lord, pause now and tell Him why you are not ready.

_____

_____

Your time, your energy, any supposed sacrifice—all that you commit to this battle—is an investment that will last for eternity. How does that make you feel?

_____

_____

At our Adventist World Radio offices we received a letter from a person living in a country of strong religious intolerance. The letter went something like this: "In all my life, I never knew there was any other religion other than Hinduism and Buddhism, but you have introduced me to Jesus Christ. Thank you for allowing me to *taste the sweetness of God.*"

> *"Oh, taste and see that the Lord is good; blessed is the man who trusts in Him!*
> *Oh, fear the Lord, you His saints! There is no want to those who fear Him.*
> *The young lions lack and suffer hunger; but those who seek the Lord*
> *shall not lack any good thing" (Ps. 34:8-10).*

Are you tasting His sweetness on a daily basis? Explain your answer in detail:

_____

_____

_____

"Our growth in grace, our joy, our usefulness—all depend upon our union with Christ. It is by communion with Him, daily, hourly—by abiding in Him—that we are to grow in grace. He is not only the author, but the finisher of our faith. It is Christ first and last and always. He is to be with us, not only at the beginning and the end of our course, but at every step of the way" (The Faith I Live By, p. 125).

➡ **Taking time with the Lord.** Someone once said, "I've learned that everyone wants to live on top of the mountain, but all the happiness and growth occur while you're climbing it." Just because you haven't made it to the mountaintop of your Christian experience yet doesn't mean you can't be happy. In prayer, thank the Lord for helping you make this climb and for being with you every step of the way.

> *"Those who will search the Scriptures for themselves, because it is the Word of God, who are willing to dig for the truth as for hidden treasures, will receive for their prize that wisdom which cometh from God. If they will not rely upon their own smartness, and not trust in their own inventions and their supposed fruitful minds, if they will give the working of the mind into the Lord's hands, and yoke up with Jesus Christ, they will not take steps where Jesus does not lead the way."*

_____

*Sermons and Talks, vol. 1, p. 285.

10

Fruitful Abiding

"At that day you will know that I am in My Father, and you in Me, and I in you."
—John 14:20

The disciples were not good enough to be invited to enter the schools of the rabbis, but as some of them were tending to their fishing nets on the beach that day, a call came from the greatest Teacher the world has ever known. Even though He had no home and no visible means of support, and the established church was suspicious of Him, the fishermen left their former profession and followed the call of this Galilean rabbi to become "fishers of men."

These men in training crisscrossed the rugged countryside aiding the Master in the task of lifting humanity from the slough of despair. They walked countless dusty miles in their worn sandals to catch every word that proceeded from the mouth of Jesus—as He shared the hope and joy of eternal life with the hungering masses. Still, it took almost three and a half years of walking by Christ's side before truth eventually found a home within the hearts of these trainees.

Although I couldn't find the source of the original quote, it is said that in the fifth century Augustine wrote of Christ's ascension from the point of view of His disciples: "You ascended from before our eyes. We turned back grieving, only to find You in our hearts."

Tangible results from this abiding presence of God were seen almost immediately. The book of Acts records that thousands upon thousands of people flooded into the church in response to the fervent pleas given by these once-abrasive and uncouth fishermen (and tax collectors and so on). It becomes evident when the abiding presence of God inhabits one's life—an abundant harvest is the result.

During the time of Christ a call was typically extended to follow a rabbi, and from that day forward the student never left his side. It was said that he followed his teacher so closely that the dust from the feet of his master would fall upon him.

Likewise, you have received the call from Rabbi Jesus to follow Him. I urge you to walk so closely to your Master that the ancient saying "May the dust of your Rabbi fall upon you" becomes your reality.

The Heavenly Gardener

"He who has My commandments and keeps them, it is he who loves Me.
And he who loves Me will be loved by My Father,
and I will love him and manifest Myself to him."
—John 14:21

If you're a Christian, you are already aware of God's desire to provide you with the beautiful robe of Christ's righteousness. This covering immediately provides you with a spotless exterior. But a close examination into the first two verses of John 15, which we looked at yesterday, reveals another side of our heavenly Father.

Today you'll be studying how your interior transformation is to take place.

Every fiber of your being will be interlaced on a cellular level with "parent stock," absorbing the ever-so-precious life-giving nutrients—constantly bathing your spiritual genetics with light, peace, goodness, happiness, and all that is wonderful. Like every good farmer, when the Father has performed His task, He expects to receive a bountiful harvest from the one whom He has been tending.

➡ **Read Galatians 5:22, 23.** What is the expected harvest you produce when you're connected to the True Vine?

_____

_____

_____

What is the number of fruit? _____

How many different flavors does the fruit of the Spirit produce? _____

The Spirit has *one* fruit but *many* flavors, somewhat like the tree of life, which is a single tree that produces 12 different varieties of fruit over a 12-month period. You see, with God all things are truly possible!

> *"To him who overcomes I will give to eat from the tree of life,*
> *which is in the midst of the Paradise of God"* (Rev. 2:7).

> *"In the middle of its street . . . was the tree of life, which bore twelve fruits,*
> *each tree yielding its fruit every month. The leaves of the tree*
> *were for the healing of the nations"* (Rev. 22:2).

Would you like to produce the fruit of the Spirit? If so, you must allow the Vinedresser access to every twig, leaf, and vine of your "life tree" in order for Him to prune what He deems necessary to produce the maximum harvest. You cannot say to God that any area is off limits.

➡ **Read John 15:1, 2.** How important is the pruning process and how does it relate to the amount of fruit you ultimately produce? (Check all that apply.)

☐ I believe pruning is a must for my life.

☐ I'm not sure it is needed.

☐ If there were no pruning, many useless twigs, leaves, and vines would be sapping strength needed elsewhere.

- ☐ It can be painful, but it is needed.
- ☐ other: _____

I happened on an interesting interview conducted by a fellow calling himself Trevor. It took place in March 2010 and is inserted as a blog by the Cork Board in Napa Valley.

Trevor interviewed an expert on vines and grapes, Josh Anstey of St. Supéry Vineyards. I selected just a couple of points to provide you with an idea of the science and care involved in pruning and also took the liberty to edit the conversation for my purposes here:

Cork Board: What is the approach you take to vineyard pruning? What impact does pruning have on the end product?

Anstey: It always depends on the variety, soil, aspect, terrain, and what we want to achieve. Pruning has a *huge* impact; it sets up the vines for the coming year and really for decades. It dictates canopy shape and the number of buds and, therefore, yields for the year.

Cork Board: In general, when does pruning happen in Napa Valley?

Anstey: You can prune anytime; after leaves drop is typical. We wait as long as we can until January, February, and March. . . . It delays bud break, and it's better for a fungus called *Eutypa lata*, plus there are less spores late in winter and juices start flowing, pushing spores from pruning wounds.

According to the interview, what is needed to produce high-quality grapes and a large yield? _____

_____

Does the Father need to "prune" you? Select the best answers. (You can choose several.)

- ☐ Pruning is necessary to the health of the vine.
- ☐ The cutting of branches can be painful, but it's needed when applied to my life.
- ☐ I'm happy that God loves me enough to take the time to trim me so I will flourish.
- ☐ My life is His to do with however He decides is best.
- ☐ I'd rather He not trim the dead branches in my life at this time, but I do trust Him.
- ☐ other: _____

The purpose of pruning is to make us fruitful and blessed. God wants to plant you beside a spring of eternal water and make you like Joseph. *"Joseph is a fruitful [vine], even a fruitful [vine] by a well; whose branches run over the wall"* (Gen. 49:22, KJV).

➡ **Write in your name in the blanks below:**

"_____ shall be like a tree planted by the rivers of water, that brings forth its fruit in its season, whose leaf also shall not wither; and whatever _____ does shall prosper" (Ps. 1:3).

➡ **Read Isaiah 5:1, 2, 4.** What happened to the vines in that vineyard?

_____

_____

_____

Fruit production is not an optional exercise of the vine but a by-product of being connected to the parent stock. It is about choice—your choice. You must choose to get connected to the heavenly Plant. This takes time, energy, and commitment!

Select your choices:

- ☐ I'll be happy to spend a little time in prayer after I watch TV.
- ☐ I'll check my e-mail and then study and pray.
- ☐ Let me just browse Google first, Lord.
- ☐ My job is so demanding that I just don't have time for You, Lord.
- ☐ Every day, I am setting aside uninterrupted time for prayer.
- ☐ There is nothing more important in my life than spending time with You and in Your Word, Lord.
- ☐ I want You to prune away everything that is not needed in my life.
- ☐ Do everything You must to connect me to You and *keep* me connected!
- ☐ other: _____

The Father promises to take wonderful care of you. He does this so He may be glorified.

➡ **Write your name in the blank spaces below:**

"If _____ will indeed obey My voice and keep My covenant, then _____ shall be a special treasure to Me above all the people; for all the earth is Mine" (Ex. 19:5).

"_____ shall . . . be righteous; _____ shall inherit the land forever, the branch of My planting, the work of My hands, that I may be glorified" (Isa. 60:21).

Commenting on John 15:1-27, the *Summarized Bible* shares this beautiful thought: "Jesus is the true vine, in which the life of believers, as abiding branches, is hid. Abiding in Him, the believer is able to walk in purity of life, with Christ sharing in all the interests of his life, taking all burdens to Him, and drawing all wisdom and strength from Him. It is only the abiding life that bears fruit to the glory of the Father" (*Complete Summary of the New Testament* [Bible Institute of Los Angeles, 1919], p. 33).

➡ **Taking time with the Lord.** In your encounter with God today, is there something that He shared with you? Pray for His guidance to remind you, and write it down:

_____

_____

_____

_____

> "He who has My commandments and keeps them,
> it is he who loves Me. And he who loves Me will be loved by My Father,
> and I will love him and manifest Myself to him."

TSG-5

All Is Not Joy

"He began to teach them that the Son of Man must suffer many things,
and be rejected by the elders and chief priests and scribes,
and be killed, and after three days rise again."
—Mark 8:31

"If thou art willing to suffer no adversity, how wilt thou be the friend of Christ?"
—Thomas à Kempis

The wise man built his house upon the rock, but he experienced the same rain, floods, and strong winds—trials came to him as they did to everyone else. The only difference between the two groups is found in the planning and construction of the foundation, but everybody went through the storm.

➡ **Read Matthew 7:24-29. Please note that *everyone* involved in the building project and the cataclysmic storm *was a church member.*** No one was exempted from trial!

The missionary Joanne Shetler writes, "God never said doing His will would be easy; He only said it would be worth it."

Were you expecting the trials of life to disappear when you became a follower of Christ?

_____

I remember Cliff as if it were just yesterday. I walked into his shop to make a purchase, and he stopped me to ask, "Jim, you always seem so happy; why is that?" I shared my faith with him, and it wasn't long before he and his wife, Beverly, were attending our church. Janene and I had many Bible studies with them as they continued in faithful fellowship.

Cliff, however, was never happy because of ongoing trials in his life. I tried to talk with him about keeping his eyes focused upon Jesus. God, I said, would see him through the problems and trials he and Beverly were facing, specifically her many medical issues.

But he could never shake the misperception that when he became a Christian, all the problems and trials of life would disappear. The two finally walked away from God because of this fatal misconception.

Read John 16:1-33. Seek God's guidance as you read along. Then, after you finish, describe what you sense God is sharing with you in His Word: _____

_____

_____

_____

*"I do not pray that You should take them out of the world, but that You should keep them
from the evil one. They are not of the world, just as I am not of the world. Sanctify them
by Your truth. Your word is truth. As You sent Me into the world, I also have sent them into the world.
And for their sakes I sanctify Myself, that they also may be sanctified by the truth"* (John 17:15-19).

At the time Jesus spoke these words to His Father, He was on His way to the Garden of Gethsemane—prepared to endure the worst trial that anyone in the history of humanity has ever had to face. Jesus, who had the closest relationship with God the Father, was not removed from trials. He went through them, and He expects us to go through them too.

The apostle Paul prayed three times that the Lord would remove his "thorn in the flesh" from him. In the following passage, underline what Paul was asking God to do:

"A thorn in the flesh was given to me, a messenger of Satan to buffet me,
lest I be exalted above measure. Concerning this thing I pleaded with the Lord three times
that it might depart from me" (2 Cor. 12:7, 8).

But notice God's answer to this great apostle and warrior of Jesus Christ. In the following scripture, underline God's response to Paul's request:

"And He said to me, 'My grace is sufficient for you, for My strength is made perfect in weakness' "
(verse 9).

Now underline the reason below for Paul's acceptance of God's will for him.

"Therefore most gladly I will rather boast in my infirmities, that the power of Christ
may rest upon me. Therefore I take pleasure in infirmities, in reproaches, in needs, in persecutions,
in distresses, for Christ's sake. For when I am weak, then I am strong" (verses 9, 10).

When you pray for comfort God gives you the Comforter. Jesus said, *"Nevertheless I tell you the truth. It is to your advantage that I go away; for if I do not go away, the Helper will not come to you; but if I depart, I will send Him to you"* (John 16:7). The presence of God is the greatest of all gifts!

James understood this reality also:

"Blessed is the man who endures temptation; for when he has been approved,
he will receive the crown of life which the Lord has promised to those who love Him" (James 1:12).

The trials and troubles of this world are the means by which God refines and transforms your character. Each trial helps to cut away the deadwood, reshapes the crooked path, improves the spiritual strength, sharpens the heavenly intellect, and fits you to live in the company of holy beings for eternity.

➡ **Write your name into the following promise:**

"I know how to be abased, and I know how to abound. Everywhere and in all things I have learned both to be full and to be hungry, both to abound and to suffer need. I _____ can do all things through Christ who strengthens me" (Phil. 4:12, 13).

Check the appropriate box:
☐ I give God my life to do as He wishes.
☐ Lord, make me willing to be made willing.
☐ other: _____

➡ **Taking time with the Lord.** If you have given God control over your life through every trial and affliction, thank Him now for giving you the strength to pass through and remain faithful in obedience. If you are suffering through a trial right now, God wants to help you; all you have to do is to ask. Do that now in prayer.

Glowing for God

"This little light of mine, I'm going to let it shine."
—Harry Dixon Loes

"In Him was life, and the life was the light of men."
—John 1:4

Would you like to be a loving person? Do you want to have joy and peace in your heart? Most of us could use a good dose of patience as well, along with some kindness and goodness. And I doubt that anyone would complain if they were given an extra measure of faithfulness. I could always use an additional dash of gentleness and self-control—couldn't you?

I *had just finished writing* the above paragraph about the fruit of the Spirit when my wife and I landed at an airport in Canada. While going through customs, we ran into two immigration agents who were having a really bad day. When asked why I was coming into Canada, I said, "I'm speaking at a Christian camp meeting in the north somewhere."

Apparently that was the wrong answer! For the next half hour we were deluged with questions that included every subject you could imagine—except maybe what I had for dinner two weeks earlier. We had had an easier time entering Cuba! My jaw soon began to tighten, and my dear wife did little better in the gentleness and self-control category. It's one thing to write about the fruit of the Spirit; it's quite another to experience it.

That's why transformation needs to be understood as a growing process in which we are continually taught to make more room for the Holy Spirit in our lives.

List three character traits present in your life that you would like God to remove and have replaced by the fruit of the Spirit:

- _____
- _____
- _____

To overcome these traits, it is an absolute necessity to have the Holy Spirit in full measure. Nor is the fruit of the Spirit free; it will cost you everything. You must surrender 100 percent—not one percentage point less!

But it's definitely worth it! It's exciting to realize that when the Holy Spirit abides in you, your old character traits are shoved out of your life by the new fruit. There is no room for both!

By God's grace you have been experiencing spiritual change—growth—during the past 10 weeks of study and prayer. Transformation in you is becoming reality! These changes are seen by others in your fruit-bearing. So as you continue to study, pray, and walk with the Lord, the Light will radiate from you—brighter and brighter each day! And people will recognize that you have been with God.

Glowing for God

I discovered the Lord was working in the heart of a fellow with whom I'd come in contact, so I began talking with him about spiritual things on a regular basis. I was so excited about Christ and what He had been doing in my life that, on one occasion, I invited him to share the same experience with Jesus that I was enjoying.

I will never forget his response—even before I finished speaking, he exclaimed, "Jim, every time you talk about God, you actually glow. I can see a light shining around you." Needless to say, I was taken aback by his assessment, but it does make sense when you consider the time Moses went up the mountain to meet God.

➡ **Fill in the blanks below:**

"Now the Lord _____ in the cloud and _____ [Moses] there, and proclaimed the name of the Lord. And the Lord _____ him and proclaimed, 'The Lord, the Lord God, merciful and gracious, longsuffering, and abounding in goodness and truth, keeping mercy for thousands, forgiving iniquity and transgression and sin, by no means clearing the guilty. . . .' So Moses made haste and bowed his head toward the earth, and _____" (Ex. 34:5-8).

"[Moses] was _____ forty days and forty nights" (verse 28).

"Then Moses came down from Mount Sinai. In his hands he was carrying the two stone tablets of the agreement. But Moses did not know that his face was shining because _____ with the Lord. . . . Aaron and all the people of Israel saw that Moses' face was shining. So they were afraid to go near him" (verses 29, 30, ICB).

"When Moses came down from Mount Sinai . . . [he] did not know that the skin of his face shone while _____. So when Aaron and all the children of Israel saw Moses, behold, the skin of his face shone, and they were afraid to come near him" (verses 29, 30).

God stepped out of heaven and met with Moses for 40 days and 40 nights. The result of this communion with God was that the face of Moses glowed with heavenly radiance. You see, you can't spend time with God and not glow for Him!

➡ **Read Daniel 12:3, Matthew 5:14-16, and Matthew 13:43.**

God wants to shine out of you, just as He did Moses!

> *"Do all things without complaining and disputing, that you may become blameless and harmless,*
> *children of God without fault in the midst of a crooked and perverse generation,*
> ***among whom you shine as lights in the world,*** *holding fast the word of life,*
> *so that I may rejoice in the day of Christ that I have not run in vain or labored in vain"* (Phil. 2:14-16).

➡ **Taking time with the Lord.** In your special time with God today, let Him know how you want to shine for Him. Let Him know about any adjustments you need to make in your life so you can glow for Him more brightly than ever before. Yes, He already knows your needs—but He wants to hear from you personally in prayer! Write down your prayer to Him below:

_____

_____

_____

_____

{ *"This little light of mine, I'm going to let it shine."* }

11

Pressing Together

Years ago Janene and I conducted a series of evangelistic meetings in Kadapa, India. We took several couples with us to help with the many logistics involved. At the time, few meetings like ours had ever been done in India, so we had very little knowledge of what to expect once we started working in the country.

Everything had been going well, except that two of the couples were quietly having some personality issues with each other. As it turned out, Ron and Pauline and the other couple were placed on a joint visitation team. That was the day they decided to visit a woman who was having spiritual troubles. No one realized just how serious her troubles were!

Upon arriving at the woman's house, the pastor who accompanied the couples asked all to leave the dwelling, except the woman, the couples, and her close friend. The two couples sat on the dirt floor in a tiny dark room holding hands in a circle of prayer. Ron began to pray, but as he prayed, the woman they were praying for grabbed his wrists and started to squeeze them.

Ron was an extremely strong man who worked in his own sawmill in Michigan, but he could not pry away her hand. Her viselike grip was hurting more by the moment! The other couple saw what was happening and, as the eyes of both couples met, they realized there were more beings in the room—they were not wrestling against flesh and blood!

Fear gripped their hearts as they immediately asked for one another's forgiveness for all the bad feelings and behavior toward one another in the past. They cried to God for help in preparation to present a united front to fight the enemy of souls.

Still in the deadly grip of the demon-possessed woman, Ron was now joined by the rest of the team in prayer. They prayed with unity of purpose to God and demanded the demon to release Ron's arm and leave the possessed woman. Immediately the demon jumped from the woman to her friend, who had been sitting silently in the corner. She, too, started to howl and scream, but again the couples demanded the demon to leave in the name of Jesus Christ. He left at their command, and peace settled upon the home and every heart present.

Never again did the two couples allow any petty problems to disrupt their mission for God. After experiencing the power of Satan, they fixed their focus steadfastly upon Christ and the work set before them.

The Promise—Waiting in Silence

"Rest in the Lord, and wait patiently for Him;
do not fret because of him who prospers in his way,
because of the man who brings wicked schemes to pass."
—Psalm 37:7

"Wait on the Lord; be of good courage, and he shall strengthen your heart."
—Psalm 27:14

I hate waiting! I don't like stoplights, traffic jams, store checkout lines, or flight delays—just to name a few. How about you? Are you patient as you wait, or are you like me?

The disciples' patience was likewise tested when the Lord *"commanded them not to depart from Jerusalem, but to wait for the Promise of the Father"* after His ascension (Acts 1:4). What promise? The answer is found in verses 5 and 8: *"You shall be baptized with the Holy Spirit not many days from now." "You shall receive power when the Holy Spirit has come upon you."*

There are many paths we could explore regarding the Master's words here, but for now we will look at just three of them: the **promise of power**, the **command to wait**, and the **promise fulfilled.**

The Promise of Power

Circle the promise in the following passage of Scripture:

*"It shall come to pass afterward that I will pour out My Spirit on all flesh;
your sons and your daughters shall prophesy, your old men shall dream dreams,
your young men shall see visions. And also on My menservants and on
My maidservants I will pour out My Spirit in those days"* (Joel 2:28, 29).

In the Gospel of John, Jesus provided a deeper understanding of the promise He gives in Acts. Below, underline those words and phrases that speak of this powerful promise and the wonderful results of its reception:

*"On the last day, . . . Jesus stood and cried out, saying, 'If anyone thirsts, let him come
to Me and drink. He who believes in Me, as the Scripture has said, out of his heart
will flow rivers of living water.' But this He spoke concerning the Spirit, whom those believing
in Him would receive; for the Holy Spirit was not yet given,
because Jesus was not yet glorified"* (John 7:37-39).

The followers of Christ had already received a measure of the Holy Spirit (John 20:22) and had experienced the results of that bestowal in many ways. But they were still to receive even greater power that would fit them for a much larger work—taking the gospel to the world.

The Command to Wait

If the disciples would trust in the Master's command, their wait would not be in vain. Their patience ended up resulting in the reception of a glorious gift—what is called the *former rain*. ("Former" because another one, the "latter," is coming before Jesus returns.) It was, indeed, a gift worth waiting for!

They waited for 10 days with no word from the Lord. How do you react when you receive no word from God?

_____

_____

An example of the silence of God is found in Matthew 15:

> *"A woman of Canaan came from that region and cried out to Him, saying,*
> *'Have mercy on me, O Lord, Son of David! My daughter is severely demon-possessed.'*
> *But He answered her not a word"* (verses 22, 23).

The woman's child was being tortured by demons and, to all appearances, Jesus did not seem to care! How would you react to Jesus' silence?

_____

_____

With God's permission, the devil hit Job hard. Satan wiped out his family and all he possessed. Then the devil slammed Job's health so hard that the poor man wished he could die. Job cried out in desperate pain. How did God answer His friend? There was no word from Him for 37 chapters! There was only gut-wrenching silence, until chapter 38, when God finally broke it.

➡ **Read Job 13:15.** Describe in your own words how Job chose to orient his life toward God.

_____

_____

Martha and Mary sent word to Jesus that Lazarus was very sick and needed the Lord's help. He had the opportunity to help His friend get better, but He did not respond until it was apparently too late!

If you have experienced the silence of God in a way like this, briefly describe it and what you now see as the results from that time in your life:

_____

_____

_____

Neither Job's faith, Martha's or Mary's faith, nor the Canaanite woman's faith faltered despite the apparent lack of response from God. They continued to hold fast to their only hope. In return, they were blessed with new life, a resurrection, and a healed child!

How is your faith? Will you continue to wait upon the Lord even when He is silent? Even when things are not going according to your plans? Will you wait patiently and faithfully for the promise of the Holy Spirit and the Lord's second coming?

> *"For the vision is yet for an appointed time; but at the end it will speak,*
> *and it will not lie. Though it tarries, wait for it; because it will surely come,*
> *it will not tarry"* (Hab. 2:3).

The Promise Fulfilled

"Suddenly there came a sound from heaven, as of a rushing mighty wind,
and it filled the whole house where they were sitting. Then there appeared to them
divided tongues, as of fire, and one sat upon each of them. And they were all
filled with the Holy Spirit and began to speak with other tongues,
as the Spirit gave them utterance" (Acts 2:2-4).

"The outpouring of the Spirit in the days of the apostles was the beginning of the early, or former, rain, and glorious was the result. To the end of time the presence of the Spirit is to abide with the true church. But near the close of earth's harvest, a special bestowal of spiritual grace is promised to prepare the church for the coming of the Son of man. This outpouring of the Spirit is likened to the falling of the latter rain; and it is for this added power that Christians are to send their petitions to the Lord of the harvest" (*The Acts of the Apostles*, pp. 54, 55).

What is going to happen according to this word? _____

When? _____

Why? _____

➡ **Taking time with the Lord.** The disciples knew that they were powerless without the promised power of the Holy Spirit. Are you willing to pray and continue to ask for His abiding presence until you receive it? Ask God right now for a greater measure of the Holy Spirit than you have ever had before!

> *"Rest in the Lord, and wait patiently for Him;*
> *do not fret because of him who prospers*
> *in his way, because of the man who brings*
> *wicked schemes to pass."*

Becoming One

"The glory which You gave Me I have given them,
that they may be one just as We are one."
—John 17:22

"Love is an act of endless forgiveness,
a tender look which becomes a habit."
—Peter Ustinov

On the day of Pentecost 12 people were baptized with "tongues of fire" as the Holy Spirit descended upon them in power. But what had they been doing for the 10 days prior to this historic experience? According to Ellen White, after Christ's ascension,

> *"His disciples—men of varied talents and capabilities—assembled in an upper chamber to pray for the gift of the Holy Spirit. In this room 'all continued with one accord in prayer and supplication.' They made thorough work of repentance by confessing their own sins. . . . Settling all differences and alienations, they were of one accord, and prayed with unity of purpose for ten days"* (*Manuscript Releases,* vol. 5, p. 368).

➡ **Describe in your own words what the disciples were doing for those 10 days:**

_____

_____

The disciples had been at odds with one another over many issues. One of the premier conflicts was deciding who was to be the greatest in the kingdom. They had become political climbers! The Lord responded to the nonsense by saying, *"Unless you are converted and become as little children, you will by no means enter the kingdom of heaven"* (Matt. 18:3).

After having completed many weeks of this transformation study, you should be more in tune with what took place in the upper room that caused the disciples, with varied personalities, ideas, and gifts, to press together and be of "one accord." **Share your thoughts on this subject:**

_____

_____

_____

If He is to be God of your entire life, He must control your relationships as well!

➡ **Read 2 Corinthians 5:17-19 and answer the questions below:**

How does Paul describe the ministry of Christ?

_____

What was the ultimate result of the upper-room prayer-and-reconciliation fest?

_____

Announcing His approval of their petitions, the Holy Spirit fell as flames of fire upon every repentant, reconciled seeker in the room that day. Finding no unconfessed sin, the flames did not consume but rather bathed the recipients in enabling power to carry the gospel to the ends of the earth. The fledging church was born through the power of the former rain!

God is now looking for people He can trust with the power of the latter rain.

➡ **Place yourself in that upper-room setting that day,** checking all that apply:

☐ I'm not sure I would have been patient enough to receive the blessing.

☐ I would have been seeking forgiveness from my fellow brethren.

☐ I would have been praying for greater blessings from God.

☐ I would have been asking Jesus to fulfill His promise of power.

☐ I would have become restless because I was missing work.

☐ I would have been uncomfortable with so many people praying for so long.

☐ I'm not sure I would have stayed the entire time.

☐ other: _____

The sound of the Spirit rushing into the house was so great that it drew a crowd of curious people. What an awesome witness of the birth of the Christian church!

"There were some religious Jews staying in Jerusalem who were from every country in the world. When they heard this noise [from heaven], a crowd came together. They were all surprised, because each one heard them speaking in his own language. They were completely amazed at this. They said, '. . . How's this possible.?'" (Acts 2:5-8, ICB).

➡ **Taking time with the Lord.** To the nonbeliever, the moving of the Spirit is always mysterious. To the believer, He is comfort, joy, and power! Do you sense the Lord speaking to you through today's study? Take time to talk with Him now and be sure to take time to listen to Him speak to you in return.

{
"The glory which You gave Me I have given them, that they may be one just as We are one."
}

Becoming One—Again!

"Call to Me, and I will answer you,
and show you great and mighty things, which you do not know."
—Jeremiah 33:3

"He stands ready to allocate His power to all who are radically dependent
on Him and radically devoted to making much of Him."
—David Platt

Of the former rain that the disciples experienced in the upper room, Ellen White wrote,

> "*These scenes are to be repeated, and with greater power. The outpouring of the Holy Spirit on the day of Pentecost was the former rain, but the latter rain will be more abundant. The Spirit awaits our demand and reception. Christ is again to be revealed in His fullness by the Holy Spirit's power. Men will discern the value of the precious pearl, and with the apostle Paul they will say, 'What things were gain to me, those I counted loss for Christ. Yea doubtless, and I count all things but loss for the excellency of the knowledge of Christ Jesus'*" (*Christ's Object Lessons*, p. 121).

What is soon to be repeated? _____

Who will receive the gift? _____

➡ **Underline the strength of the gift to be given in the quote above.**

The early upper-room experience had been one of division. Judas wanted to secure the highest position, and all were at odds with one another. This was in total opposition to the words of Jesus, who had said, "*Leave your gift there before the altar, and go your way. First be reconciled to your brother, and then come and offer your gift*" (Matt. 5:24).

As history verifies, however, once the disciples experienced the rebirth and died to self, the transformation process led them to reconcile with the others—*and then* the former rain fell.

Reconciliation

Late in their lives both my dad and mom became Christians. This was an exciting time for my wife and me, because we had been praying for them to come to Christ for more than 30 years. Their joy was evident from the beginning. They made many new friends at church and joined in financially by giving their tithe and supporting missions in other parts of the world.

There was, however, one big problem that kept cropping up in my dad's new experience—terrible feelings about his sister, who had wronged him years earlier. The hurt ran so deeply that he refused to forgive her or even speak to her. This hate had festered so long that it was poisoning him from the inside out.

But the Holy Spirit is relentless, desiring our greatest good for eternity. The Lord continued to speak to my father until, one day, in obedience to Jesus, he picked up the phone and called his sister to heal the wound. It was evident in his smile and mannerisms that the burden had been rolled away!

➡ **Are there any relationships in your life that need repairing and reconciliation? Spend time with the Lord and ask Him now.** You don't want anything coming between you and the gift of the latter rain. It is time to become like those in the early church by putting away every difference.

As you prayed, was there anyone—or any situation—God brought to your attention? Any hurt or injury that you should go and reconcile with someone? Explain below:

_____

_____

It might even be that they are wrongly holding something against you, but as Jesus' child, you should be the one to seek reconciliation—just as He did for the entire universe. Ellen White said,

> *"Oh, how many times, when I have seemed to be in the presence of God and holy angels, I have heard the angel voice saying, 'Press together, press together, press together. Do not let Satan cast his hellish shadow between brethren. Press together; in unity there is strength.' I repeat the message to you. . . . Be determined that you will press together; seek God with all the heart, and you will find Him, and the love of Christ, that passeth understanding, will come into your hearts"* (*Selected Messages*, book 2, p. 374).

Many people think they have no part in the reconciliation process if they are not the ones at fault, but remember, Jesus was not at fault! Will you go and do as Jesus did? *"Let this mind be in you."* It is time to become one in preparation for the latter rain. I believe with all my heart that the Lord's return is soon, and I want to receive more of His Spirit—**how about you?**

_____

In Unit 9 you studied the idea of living in the Spirit. As followers of God, we have been given a measure of the Spirit to enable us to walk with Him. However, near the close of earth's history, there is more to come for those who hunger and thirst for it!

> *"The great work of the gospel is not to close with less manifestation of the power of God than marked its opening. . . . God has a work for His people to do for the world, and if they will work in harmony with one another and with heaven, He will demonstrate His power in their behalf as He did for His first disciples on the day of Pentecost"* (*The Faith I Live By*, p. 332).

➡ **Think about it: God never withdrew the former rain from His followers!** That power is still with us to this day, and until we avail ourselves of this gift to its fullest, we shall not receive the additional gift of the latter rain.

Janene and I had been attending a weekly study group for sometime, and God was working upon our hearts in a powerful way. The Lord was pressing me with conviction; I wanted more of Him—a deeper relationship, a closeness . . . I yearned to experience more of Him!

But when I suggested to the group that we pray for the outpouring of the Holy Spirit, I was met with strong resistance. I couldn't understand it. "Why don't you want more of God?" I asked. The rebuff went something like this: "We are already children of God! Don't you believe we have the Holy Spirit now? Why do you want to ask for what we already have?"

What category of believers do you fit into? Do you want more of God—or are you satisfied with the experience you have now? Explain:

_____

_____

Months later we found a mountain retreat near a beautiful Oregon lake for the group to spend time in prayer and fellowship. During the weekend I continued to seek the group's agreement regarding prayer for more of God's Spirit and, finally, everyone acquiesced—mainly to keep me quiet!

It had been a long time coming, but with one heart we petitioned God for His mighty blessings in the form of the Holy Spirit. He answered in such a rich and powerful way that everyone—to a person—in our group recognized that God had filled the believers in that cabin with His Spirit of love and power!

We each learned that united prayer is the key:

> "Since this is the means by which we are to receive power, why do we not hunger and thirst for the gift of the Spirit? Why do we not talk of it, pray for it, and preach concerning it? The Lord is more willing to give the Holy Spirit to those who serve Him than parents are to give good gifts to their children. For the daily baptism of the Spirit every worker should offer his petition to God" (*The Acts of the Apostles*, p. 50).

How often should we petition God for the Holy Spirit? _____

Never be satisfied with the measure of God you have at present in your life! There is always room for more. Test what I have said and see for yourself. The Holy Spirit is the greatest power source in the universe for transforming you.

> "The Lord is more willing to give the Holy Spirit to those who serve Him than parents are to give good gifts to their children" (*ibid.*).

Check the answer that best fits you:

☐ I am more aware of the presence of God in my life than ever before.

☐ I am aware of an absence of God and desire more.

☐ I am beginning to discover that God wants to give me more of Himself.

☐ other: _____

➡ **Taking time with the Lord:** Seek God's blessing in prayer, asking Him for all of the Holy Spirit you can hold. Patiently wait upon Him if He seems to tarry, but continue to press your petition to His throne, seeking the blessing that will bring all other blessings in its train.

{ *"Call to Me, and I will answer you, and show you great and mighty things, which you do not know."* }

Identifying God at Work

"By this we know that we abide in Him, and He in us,
because He has given us of His Spirit."
—1 John 4:13

"If you want the fire of God, you must become the fuel of God."
—Tommy Tenney

"Let Christians put away all dissension and give themselves to God for the saving of the lost. Let them ask in faith for the promised blessing, and it will come. The outpouring of the Spirit in the days of the apostles was 'the former rain,' and glorious was the result. But the latter rain will be more abundant. What is the promise to those living in these last days? 'Turn you to the stronghold, ye prisoners of hope: even today do I declare that I will render double unto thee'" (Counsels for the Church, *p. 98*).

As we've read before, when the disciples walked out of the upper room, the crowds had already begun to gather because of the rushing, tornado-like sound that brought the fire of the Holy Spirit. Set on fire by God, they were ready to take advantage of where God was working as they viewed the ever-expanding crowd.

Are you able to identify God at work in and around your everyday life?

- ☐ Yes, on a regular basis.
- ☐ Not usually.
- ☐ I'm unsure.
- ☐ No.
- ☐ other: _____

How did Jesus know what to do? He studied Scripture and talked with the Father constantly. Henry Blackaby, in his study guide *Experiencing God*, aptly summarizes the relationship of Jesus to the Father as follows:

- The Father has been working right up until now.
- Now He has me working.
- I do nothing on my own initiative.
- I watch to see what the Father is doing.
- I do what I see the Father already doing.
- You see, the Father loves me.
- He shows me everything that He Himself is doing.

Who is the example we must follow? _____

Is there anything in the list that you have a problem applying to your life in relationship to Jesus? If so, what is it?

_____

God is always at work around you, and when He wants you to join Him, He reveals where He is working. That is your invitation to join Him at work. And when He reveals to you that He is at work, it answers this question for you: "Lord, when do You want me to start?" When God reveals where He is at work, join Him!

An Impatient Shepherd

Moses thought he was the promised deliverer, so he went out and killed an Egyptian. He didn't deliver anyone, but instead only ended up having to flee for his life!

After 40 years in the desert tending to sheep, he learned to be dependent upon God and not formulate his own plans. He was now material through which God could work miracles.

The Lord appeared to Moses in a burning bush and said, "I have an ongoing work. I am delivering the children of Israel, and I would like you to join Me in that work." You see, this was all about God and His plans, not the plans of Moses.

Now Moses had to decide if he was going to stay where he was or follow God's leading. This is always the case when God calls you to service for His work—around the block or around the world.

And you can't stay where you are and go with God. You must separate from the world and follow God's directions for your life. Moses did, and a nation of more than a million people was delivered without losing a single soul!

Abram is also a prime example of following God where He is working. God revealed to Abram that He was building a great nation and invited the faithful servant to join Him in nation-building. It meant pulling up stakes at 70-plus years old and going to a land yet unrevealed to him, but Abram accepted God's invitation to join Him—and he was abundantly blessed.

Can you think of other examples in the Bible where God was at work?

_____

Has God revealed to you where He is working this time around you?
1. _____
2. _____
3. _____

Let's assume that you travel the subway to work each day. On one particular morning the person sitting next to you is reading the newspaper. After passing a stop or two, the person turns to you, folds their newspaper, and says, "Wow, the world is falling apart! I wonder if the Bible is true." What would that tell you? God has revealed to you that He is at work in the heart of this person! That is your *invitation* to join Him at *work*. The question is What do you do now?

Check the box that best indicates your response to God:
- ☐ I must get to work, so I might offer a quick "Yes, it is true."
- ☐ It's my stop, and I'm late to work . . . I say nothing.
- ☐ I hand the person my card and say, "If you would like to know more, e-mail me."
- ☐ I know I will miss my stop and be late for work, but I respond, "Yes, I've discovered the Bible to be accurate. Would you like to know more? Knowing has made a wonderful difference in my life."
- ☐ other: _____

If you will open your life to the Holy Spirit, He will reveal to you where God is working. He did it for Jesus, and He will do the same for you.

➡ **Read Matthew 16:13-17. Notice what the Lord showed Peter.** Any time there is the activity of God in the life of a believer or nonbeliever, it is because of the working of the Holy Spirit. We need to train our minds to see the activity of God and watch for the evidence of that working as it unfolds around us.

Janene and I had been attending camp meeting in a picturesque country setting. Driving toward the camp one day on a narrow dirt road, we saw a truck towing a camper approaching us. We thought it could be a couple we met at camp who was leaving that day, so we pulled over to wait for them. As they came closer, we saw it was not the couple we were expecting, but we felt led to wait for whoever it was to say goodbye and to ask God to go with them in their journey. As it turned out, it was a young couple whom I had briefly visited earlier in the week.

As they drove away, Janene said, "Well, I wonder what purpose God had in setting up that meeting." Shortly after we returned home, I received an e-mail from the couple telling us how special our brief conversation with them had been. They were considering becoming missionaries and were seeking God's guidance. I entered into an e-mail dialogue with them and offered them additional words of encouragement as they sought God's will for their lives. Some would say that encounter was mere chance, but when you allow God to guide your life, there are no "just-chance" situations.

Can you think of your own examples of where you have seen, or do see, God at work?

1. _____
2. _____
3. _____

Pick one of these encounters and describe how you knew it was God at work:

_____
_____
_____

Did you list a baptism as one of your examples? Or perhaps someone entering into Bible studies? These activities would not occur without God being at work in their lives. *"No one can come to Me unless the Father who sent Me draws him"* (John 6:44).

As you grow in your understanding of how God works and become better able to see Him at work, your life will take on a new and exciting dimension.

But you might be saying, "I have trouble seeing God at work!" Remember when God created Adam? He used the dust of the earth to form and fashion the new human being. As a reconciled child of the King, the Creator will remake you so that you can see Him and recognize where He is at work.

"He spat on the ground and made clay with the saliva; and He anointed the eyes of the blind man with the clay" (John 9:6). A blind man came to Jesus for healing, so the Lord took the dust of the earth, spit in it, and created new eyes for the blind man. There is nothing that the Holy Spirit cannot do for you to enable you to join Him in God's work—if you ask Him.

> *"I counsel you to buy from Me gold refined in the fire, that you may be rich;*
> *and white garments, that you may be clothed, that the shame of your nakedness*
> *may not be revealed; and anoint your eyes with eye salve, **that you may see**"* (Rev. 3:18).

One of the many problems with the Laodicean church is its massive spiritual blindness to the conditions around them and the conditions of their own hearts, but the application of the Holy Spirit can take care of this problem in our lives and in our churches. But we have to be made willing, and we have to ask in prayerful submission with our brethren.

➡ **Taking time with the Lord.** The Bible says, *"You have an anointing from the Holy One"* (1 John 2:20). The Holy Spirit is the answer to all of your needs and desires. Ask God to rain upon you with mighty measures of His Spirit, to anoint your eyes so you can behold Him at work. And when you see Him working in lives all around you, ask God to give you the courage to join Him!

Joining God at Work

"He who serves Christ in these things is acceptable
to God and approved by men."
—Romans 14:18

"The Lord added to the church daily those who were being saved."
—Acts 2:47

Have you ever read how many new souls were added to the church during the initial proclamation of the gospel by the new Christians? It's extraordinary!

➡ **Read the following texts and list the numbers where applicable:**

Acts 2:41 _____

Acts 4:4 _____

Verse 32 _____

Acts 2:47 _____

Acts 4:31 _____

Jesus said, *"Behold, I say to you, lift up your eyes and look at the fields, for they are already white for harvest!"* (John 4:35). It was true then, and it is true now: the harvest is massive *and* God is calling you to join Him at work. You can impact the world for God if He is abiding in you. And if He is in you, sharing Jesus with others will become your biggest desire! Working to reach others is part of the total transformation process we've been studying.

➡ **Read John 5:17-20. Jesus is to be our example in all things. As He followed the Father, so we are to follow Him. In the texts below, underline what Jesus is asking you—His disciple—to do:**

*"If anyone serves Me, let him follow Me; and where I am, there My servant will be also.
If anyone serves Me, him My Father will honor"* (John 12:26).

"He who does not take his cross and follow after Me is not worthy of Me" (Matt. 10:38).

"Follow Me, and I will make you fishers of men" (Matt. 4:19).

*"If anyone desires to come after Me, let him deny himself, and take up his cross,
and follow Me"* (Matt. 16:24).

"My sheep hear My voice, and I know them, and they follow Me" (John 10:27).

You can't stay where you are if you are to go with God. And because He says, *"Follow Me, and I will make you a fisher of men,"* it means that fishing for men and women is not optional. It is an outgrowth of the Holy Spirit taking possession of you—it is part of transformation. If you are not fishing, you are going nowhere!

"What was the result of the outpouring of the Spirit upon the Day of Pentecost? The glad tidings of a risen Savior

were carried to the utmost bounds of the inhabited world. The hearts of the disciples were surcharged with a benevolence so full, so deep, so far-reaching, that it impelled them to go to the ends of the earth, testifying: 'God forbid that I should glory, save in the cross of our Lord Jesus Christ.' . . . As they proclaimed the truth as it is in Jesus, hearts yielded to the power of the message. The church beheld converts flocking to her from all directions. Backsliders were reconverted. Sinners united with Christians in seeking the pearl of great price. Those who had been the bitterest opponents of the gospel became its champions" (Counsels for the Church, p. 99).

"Christ has made provision that His church shall be a transformed body, illumined with the light of heaven, possessing the glory of Immanuel. It is His purpose that every Christian shall be surrounded with a spiritual atmosphere of light and peace. There is no limit to the usefulness of the one who, putting self aside, makes room for the working of the Holy Spirit upon his heart and lives a life wholly consecrated to God" (ibid.).

Select the following choices that fit you best:

☐ I am too scared to witness.

☐ I like sharing my faith with others.

☐ I've never really shared my faith, but I am willing to try.

☐ That's not my gift.

☐ If God helps me, I'm ready to let Him work through me.

☐ other: _____

"I am only one, but still I am one. I cannot do everything, but still I can do something; and because I cannot do everything, I will not refuse to do something that I can do."—Helen Keller.

Pam and Dan have been our good friends for years. They've experienced many of the spiritual trials and problems that Janene and I went through—and some of them we even went through together.

I don't think Pam would mind me telling you that for years she found it difficult to share her faith because her experience with the Lord was lukewarm at best. But she finally grabbed on to God with all of her will and strength and started the transformation journey.

Some time ago we were talking with Pam, and she excitedly shared that she and a friend were conducting a Bible study with someone. She shared every detail of how the study was going. What a change!—Janene and I almost fell over. That's the power of God working in the life of His child, for sure.

Pam was years into her transformation journey before she gave her first Bible study, but it certainly wasn't her last. What an amazing God we serve! He will take you where you are and lead you each day, step by step, up the ladder of transformation and eternal life.

"Oh that Christ's followers might realize that it is not houses and lands, bank-stock or wheat-fields, or even life itself, that is now at stake; but souls for whom Christ died!" (*Review and Herald*, Jan. 19, 1886).

The Dead Sea lies between Israel and Jordan. It is more than 1,300 feet below sea level—the lowest point on the earth. Vital nutrients designed by the Creator to provide life to the planet flow downward into this basin and become trapped. What was meant to bring life stagnates and eventually dies.

Likewise, in order to have life, you must share what God is sharing with you or you will stagnate spiritually. If He desires to bring life to someone today through you, are you, as a follower of Christ, willing to let Him lead you to that person? _____

She Had a Willing Heart

Janelle had just graduated from college and was living in Boston. Her family planned to come visit her and to celebrate her birthday, which was December 29. They left the day prior to her birthday, however, and she was alone in the big city. What would she do? She prayed, "God, how can I spend my birthday with You?"

That very night the Lord gave her a dream in which she was directed to purchase 12 red roses and walk through the city handing them out. She woke up knowing that she must do as the dream directed, but the only money she had was her birthday money—a gift for her to purchase a pair of New Balance running shoes.

After she found the roses, what seemed to be the last bunch in the city, she headed to the train station. She then began to ask God who should receive the roses and, throughout the day, she was guided to one person after another. Each recipient was blessed and thrilled to receive a rose from Janelle, but the best was yet to come!

Eleven roses were gone; one beautiful rose remained—and Janelle had no idea what to do with it. As she prayed for guidance, she was walking past a hospital and had the urge to go inside to the nurses' station. There she inquired, "Do you have a patient who would like a rose?"

"I can't believe you are here," the duty nurse answered. "Phillip is dying, so please go right on in."

Janelle entered the room to find Phillip, with eight people surrounding his bed. They never said a word as she walked up to the dying man. He saw the rose and began to cry. She said, "I have been looking for you all day long," and she handed him the rose. He said something softly in Spanish as she left.

A woman came running out of the room calling for her and said, "How did you know?" Before Janelle could say anything, the woman hugged her and began to cry. You see, the dying request of Phillip to this woman, who was a volunteer Spanish translator for the hospital, was to have a red rose. She explained that she had been so busy that day translating throughout the hospital, she was never able to purchase the rose to fulfill his dying wish. Then Janelle suddenly showed up and delivered his perfect red rose!

Janelle then related to the woman her story of God's leading. The stranger asked what she was going to do next. "I'm going to go by the New Balance store and look at a pair of shoes." But she had used all her money on roses, so she could only look and dream.

The woman replied, "You don't know who I am, do you?"

"No," Janelle answered.

"I'm the executive vice president of New Balance Shoes. Tomorrow I'm going to take you to meet my president and then to our warehouse, where you are going to pick out whatever pair of running shoes you want!"

Blessings Await Those Who Listen to the Master Fisherman

When you join God at work, you never know where He will lead you—and what blessings await you. But you can also rest assured that the fishing will be good and the blessings will be sweet.

> *"[Jesus] said to Simon, 'Launch out into the deep and let down your nets for a catch.'*
> *But Simon answered and said to Him, 'Master, we have toiled all night and caught nothing;*
> *nevertheless at Your word I will let down the net.' And when they had done this,*
> *they caught a great number of fish, and their net was breaking. . . .*
> *He and all who were with him were astonished at the catch of fish*
> *which they had taken"* (Luke 5:4-9).

And again Jesus told the disciples where to fish for the best catch:

> *"Jesus said to them, 'Children, have you any food?' They answered Him,*
> *'No.' And He said to them, 'Cast the net on the right side of the boat,*
> *and you will find some.' So they cast, and now they were not able to draw it in*
> *because of the multitude of fish"* (John 21:5, 6).

When you choose to be led by God, you don't need to be concerned about success. The Master will deal with that. Are you ready to fish for the Master? _____

I love to plant a little garden each season and watch it grow. My space is too small to plant much, so I typically keep it to tomatoes, beans, cucumbers, and a few other items. But one year I planted potatoes because I wanted to see how big the potatoes would get. For a while, however, all I could see were the green tops. It was so tempting to pull up the plants and check out the growth, but I knew that doing this before their time would kill them. I needed to be patient!

You need to be patient as well. Don't become frustrated with your experience but allow God to grow you—just as He grew Pam into a fisher of men. Your part is to make sure that you are planted in God's garden and are allowing Him the daily opportunity to take care of the rest.

➡ **Taking time with the Lord.** Thank the Creator in prayer for allowing you to grow and flourish as you become a channel of His blessings to those around you and gather the willing into the fold of God—your new neighbors for eternity! Ask Him to continue growing your life each day.

> *"He who serves Christ in these things is acceptable to God and approved by men."*

12

Step by Step—Becoming New

"Man cannot discover new oceans unless he has the courage to lose sight of the shore."
—*André Gide*

The apostle Paul shared this wonderful promise: *"If anyone is in Christ, he is a new creation; old things have passed away; behold, all things have become new"* (2 Cor. 5:17). How many things become new? That's right—*all* of them! Every old thing is gone and is replaced by the new. The life that was once polluted by sin is to be remade into the image of Christ by the Master Craftsman Himself. Through Him we choose to create new habits, and soon these new habits create who we become.

Over a period of 11 weeks you have been led by the Holy Spirit to walk in new pathways. It's now time to extend and grow your walk with God into the future by continually cultivating new habits and forming new directions—living the life of transformational victory.

"Let us avail ourselves of the means provided for us that we may be transformed into His likeness, and be restored to fellowship with the ministering angels, to harmony and communion with the Father and the Son" (*Steps to Christ*, p. 22).

Long-term benefits are reserved for long-term commitments. If you haven't already done so, it's time to make extended commitments to Christ that will result in new habits—created to carry you forward into God's eternal future. This means radical commitment to your prayer life, your study life, and to your lifestyle—following His voice in all He asks of you.

"We are to be individual toilers. Character cannot be bought or sold. It is formed by patient, continuous effort. Much patience is required in the striving for that life which is to come. We may all strive for perfection of character, but all who come into possession of it will earn it step by step, by the cultivation of the virtues that God commends. The Holy Spirit presents before man the agencies provided for his transformation. If he heeds the words, 'Whosoever will come after me, let him deny himself, and take up his cross, and follow me,' he will receive help from a power that is infinite" (*Review and Herald*, May 28, 1908).

God set forth the plan for this power in the wilderness. He directed the Israelites to build a sanctuary so He could *"dwell among them."* King David showed he understood the importance of God's sanctuary when he sang, *"Your way, O God, is in the sanctuary; who is so great a God as our God?"* (Ps. 77:13).

So let's take a moment to look inside the sanctuary at its furnishings.

In the first apartment of the sanctuary we find the table of showbread; the seven-branch candlestick, fueled by oil to provide light day and night; and the altar of incense, with smoke that rose before the Lord.

This trio of power will enable you to form new habits:

- **Candlestick:** symbolizes the Holy Spirit
- **Incense:** symbolizes our prayers rising up before the Lord
- **Bread:** symbolizes Scriptures and the Living Word, Jesus Christ.

As your prayers ascend upward before the Lord's eternal throne, the Holy Spirit provides the light that leads you to discover the Bread of Life.

This pathway to transformation is visually represented by God through the wilderness sanctuary, and it is still the only pathway that will lead you step by step to God and transformation: the Holy Spirit, prayer, and Bible study.

**If you do not have a copy of *Steps to Christ,* by Ellen G. White,
please purchase a copy, as you will need it for this week's study.**

Unit 12, Day 1

Staying Connected

"Cause me to hear Your lovingkindness in the morning, for in You do I trust;
cause me to know the way in which I should walk, for I lift up my soul to You."
—Psalm 143:8

"The truths that I know best I have learned on my knees.
I never know a thing well, till it is burned into my heart by prayer."
—John Bunyan

In perhaps her most signature gospel work, *Steps to Christ,* Ellen White writes about the necessity of prayer in the Christian life:

> "The darkness of the evil one encloses those who neglect to pray. The whispered temptations of the enemy entice them to sin; and it is all because they do not make use of the privileges that God has given them in the divine appointment of prayer. Why should the sons and daughters of God be reluctant to pray, when prayer is the key in the hand of faith to unlock heaven's storehouse, where are treasured the boundless resources of Omnipotence? Without unceasing prayer and diligent watching we are in danger of growing careless and of deviating from the right path. The adversary seeks continually to obstruct the way to the mercy seat, that we may not by earnest supplication and faith obtain grace and power to resist temptation" (p. 94).

Write down how this statement applies to your personal walk with God.

_____

_____

_____

➡ **Read the following texts and write down the central theme of each one:**

Luke 6:12 _____

Matthew 14:23 _____

Mark 6:46 _____

If Jesus—our example—needed prayer, how much more prayer time do you and I need? You can never become best friends with someone if you don't spend time talking with them. That's why the devil's goal is to cut off all communication between you and the Lord.

How much dedicated time do you give in prayer with God each day? _____

Do you sense that the Lord wants to spend more time talking with you, and if so, how much more?

_____

If I spent only five minutes each day talking with my wife, we would not be married for long. Every marriage counselor knows this! How long can you maintain a relationship with God without talking?

➡ **Memorize the following fact about prayer:**

"Prayer is the key in the hand of faith to unlock heaven's storehouse, where are treasured the boundless resources of Omnipotence" (Steps to Christ, p. 94).

In Mark 9 the disciples were confronted by a demon that was in complete control of a young man. Their attempts to cast it out were utterly frustrated. When Jesus appeared on the scene, however, He didn't even raise a sweat in casting out the fallen foe. A little later the disciples came to Jesus and asked, "*'Why could we not cast it out?' So He said to them, 'This kind can come out by nothing but prayer and fasting'*" (verses 28, 29).

We cannot do battle with the devil on our own, and that's what the prayerless disciples attempted to do! Instead we are counseled to *"take the helmet of salvation, and the sword of the Spirit, which is the word of God; praying always with all prayer and supplication in the Spirit, being watchful to this end with all perseverance and supplication"* (Eph. 6:17, 18).

The Lord also tells us:

"Without faith it is impossible to please Him, for he who comes to God must believe that He is, and that He is a rewarder of those who diligently seek Him" (Heb. 11:6).

"Whatever things you ask when you pray, believe that you receive them, and you will have them" (Mark 11:24).

The thing is, however, prayer time does not happen automatically. You must plan for it! You must make a daily, conscious choice to form a new prayer habit resulting in regular quality time with God. It is true that we should always have a prayer on our lips and in our heart, but, as our Lord showed when He walked in our shoes, the more time you spend on the mountaintop in dedicated prayer, the more Holy Spirit power you will acquire.

I confess that I've had a problem with prayer for much of my life. I have difficulty maintaining focus for any length of time. But years ago I heard of prayer journaling, and it helps me focus on my prayer time. I can't say it's definitely for you, but it has sure meant a lot to me.

If you haven't done it before, give prayer journaling a try. Simply write out your prayers as a way to talk with God.

Some years ago I created an acronym—**P.R.A.Y.E.R.**—for a prayer journal printed by Amazing Facts to aid in the exciting journey of prayer. It goes like this:

Praise	Start your prayers with praise to our mighty God. (See Ps. 145.)
Repentance	We come as sinners to the throne of grace, pleading for the blood of the perfect Lamb to cleanse us from all of our sins. This is a must in our prayers. "*'Come now, and let us reason together,' says the Lord, 'though your sins are like scarlet, they shall be as white as snow; though they are red like crimson, they shall be as wool'*" (Isa. 1:18).
Ask	Ask boldly of the Lord, setting before Him the needs of those you come into contact with and for all humanity. Seek for their conversation and ultimate salvation. *"Select another and still another soul, daily seeking guidance from God, laying everything before Him in earnest prayer, and working in divine wisdom"* (Medical Ministry, p. 244). *"Let us therefore come boldly to the throne of grace, that we may obtain mercy and find grace to help in time of need"* (Heb. 4:16).
You	Seek for the outpouring of the Holy Spirit in your life and ask for power and victory to overcome every sin in your life. Desire of God every wonderful character trait so that you might become more like Him. Set before God your plans, dreams, desires, and aspirations.

Then listen for His direction. *"Everyone who asks receives, and he who seeks finds, and to him who knocks it will be opened"* (Luke 11:10).

Expect

As you approach the "E" in your prayers, you should be expecting great answers from your Friend. Remember, we should come to Him *"with no doubting, for he who doubts is like a wave of the sea driven and tossed by the wind"* (James 1:6).

Receive

Hebrews 11:6 says that *"without faith it is impossible to please Him, for he who comes to God must believe that He is, and that He is a rewarder of those who diligently seek Him."* As you daily talk with your Lord, you will receive all you need.

Give this step-by-step prayer guide a try! You might even find that you will be spending far more time with God than you have before.

Ask the Lord to wake you up earlier in order to spend more time with Him. Are you willing to test Him and see if He wants to spend more time talking with you? _____

Check all that apply to you:

☐ I will do everything I can to draw nearer to my Lord.
☐ I will ask God to wake me up earlier.
☐ I pray about an hour each day now.
☐ I hunger and thirst for more of Him.
☐ other: _____

➡ **Read *Steps to Christ*, chapter 11, "The Privilege of Prayer."**

➡ **Taking time with the Lord.** Ellen White wrote, *"Prayer is the opening of the heart to God as to a friend. Not that it is necessary in order to make known to God what we are, but in order to enable us to receive Him. Prayer does not bring God down to us, but brings us up to Him"* (*Steps to Christ*, p. 93). Talk to God about today's lesson, asking Him to help you develop a prayer life like the one Jesus had.

"Cause me to hear Your lovingkindness in the morning, for in You do I trust; cause me to know the way in which I should walk, for I lift up my soul to You."

An Audience With the Infinite One

"How can a young man cleanse his way?
By taking heed according to Your word."
—Psalm 119:9

"The Bible is God's voice speaking to us,
just as surely as though we could hear it with our ears."
—Ellen G. White*

The first three chapters of the Bible speak of Paradise lost. The last two chapters speak of Paradise restored. And all those chapters in between?—those are our instructions for how we are to regain what was lost.

We have Paradise to win and a hell to shun. Doesn't it stand to reason that we would want to read and follow the instructions God has lovingly given to us? What do you think?

"I prayed for faith, and thought that someday faith would come down and strike me like lightning. But faith did not seem to come. One day I read [in] the tenth chapter of Romans, 'Now faith cometh by hearing, and hearing by the Word of God.' I had closed my Bible, and prayed for faith. I now opened my Bible, and began to study, and faith has been growing ever since."—Dwight L. Moody.

➡ **Underline how Bible study works and its effects upon the reader:**

"The Scriptures are the great agency in this transformation of character. Christ prayed, 'Sanctify them through thy truth: thy word is truth.' . . . If studied and obeyed, the Word of God works in the heart, subduing every unholy attribute. The Holy Spirit comes to convict of sin, and the faith that springs up in the heart works by love to Christ, conforming us . . . to His will" (In Heavenly Places, p. 21).

*"The word of God is living and powerful, and sharper than any two-edged sword,
piercing even to the division of soul and spirit, and of joints and marrow,
and is a discerner of the thoughts and intents of the heart"* (Heb. 4:12).

Now contemplate the following amazing statement in relation to your spiritual journey:

"There is nothing more calculated to energize the mind and strengthen the intellect than the study of the Word of God. No other book is so potent to elevate the thoughts, to give vigor to the faculties, as the . . . ennobling truths of the Bible. If God's Word were studied as it should be, men would have a breadth of mind, a nobility of character, and a stability of purpose that are rarely seen in these times. . . . The search for truth will reward the seeker at every turn, and each discovery will open up richer fields for his investigation" (Fundamentals of Christian Education, p. 126).

➡ **Based on this counsel, list what the study of God's Word will do for you:**

1. _____

2. _____

3. _____

4. _____

5. _____

6. _____

> *"In searching the Scriptures, in feeding upon the words of life, . . . it is the voice of God to the soul. We may be confused sometimes over the voice of our friends; but in the Bible we have the counsel of God upon all important subjects which concern our eternal interests, and in temporal matters we may learn a great deal. Its teaching will be always suited to our peculiar circumstances and calculated to prepare us to endure trial and fit us for our God-given work"* (*My Life Today*, p. 283).

Paul told Timothy, *"Be diligent to present yourself approved to God, a worker who does not need to be ashamed, rightly dividing the word of truth"* (2 Tim. 2:15). If you want to be able to stand before God on that great day, you must spend time in study of His Word.

Select the statement that most closely matches your time in the Bible:

☐ I spend less than 15 minutes each day in study.

☐ I spend about a half hour per day in study.

☐ I try to spend at least one hour every day in His Word.

☐ I just don't seem to have much time to study.

☐ There are always emergencies that call me away from study.

☐ When the alarm rings, I have my hand on the doorknob and I'm gone.

☐ other: _____

Remember, Bible study, like prayer, is a choice. You must choose to spend time with God and dig deeply into His Word. Said R. C. Sproul,

> *"We fail in our duty to study God's Word not so much because it is difficult to understand, not so much because it is dull and boring, but because it is work. Our problem is not a lack of intelligence or a lack of passion. Our problem is that we are lazy."*

When Morris Venden was a young preacher, he visited the home of H.M.S. Richards, Sr., who had turned his garage into a library. It was filled top to bottom with Bibles and books—and Richards never let a spare minute go by without pulling out something to study. He was a very spiritual man who was deeply in love with his Lord and was recognized by his church as one of the foremost ministers of his time.

After the two spent some time visiting, their conversation moved to the spirituality of pastors in the church. Richards made a statement that shook Venden: "I'm afraid that our young men don't even study four hours a day." Wow! Can you imagine? The young preacher could not believe what he had just heard, but he recognized why this man of God would make such a statement.

In his older years, when Richards stood before large audiences, he would invite the people to turn to various Bible texts and then he would read. Since Richards was in love with the Bible, his messages were naturally filled with Scripture. What the audience didn't realize was that by this time in his life, Richards' eyesight was so bad that he could no longer read God's Word. Those who sat behind him on the rostrum have said that, at times, he would have his Bible upside down yet still "read" the texts perfectly. He did it all from memory!

Do you look at certain preachers and say, "I wish I could have their faith"? As a young Christian, I saw Richards as the most spiritual man I had ever met—and I yearned to be like him. I realized only later in life that God offers all of us the opportunity to become spiritual giants.

The recipe for giant-sized spirituality is to take a large amount of prayer, add to it a double portion of Bible study, and mix in a willingness to follow all you've heard and studied. To be a spiritual giant, you not only need a lot of prayer, you must spend a great deal of time in God's Word. If you do so, you will be transformed into the image of Christ—the best example of spirituality to follow!

"Your word I have hidden in my heart, that I might not sin against You" (Ps. 119:11).

Can your family, friends, and associates tell that you have been spending more time with Christ lately?

_____

For 40 years God provided food for His people in the form of "manna," which miraculously appeared on the desert floor every morning. They were to gather and eat this bread from heaven on the same day; if they held what they collected over for an extra day, it became rotten with maggots and stank. In addition, they were instructed to gather the manna before the sun became hot; otherwise, it would melt. *"They gathered it every morning, every man according to his need. And when the sun became hot, it melted"* (Ex. 16:21).

Here are some powerful correlations of God's Word—the bread of life—to the manna experience:

If they held over the manna for the following day, it rotted. Likewise, yesterday's spiritual experience is not enough to get you through today! You must have fresh bread, a fresh encounter with God each and every day.

They had to gather the manna before the sun came up, when the heat of the day became so hot that it melted. Likewise, early in the morning, before the heat of the day's trials, is the best time to study God's Word. Sit at the feet of Jesus *before* the trials and troubles crowd in and melt away the sacred time and destroy the opportunity to experience God.

How will today's study impact and guide your spiritual journey with Christ? Explain in detail:

_____

_____

_____

_____

_____

➡ **Read *Steps to Christ*, chapter 10, "A Knowledge of God."**

➡ **Taking time with the Lord.** Talk to God about today's lesson, asking Him to help you develop a Bible study habit that will grow your spiritual experience and transform you into the image of Jesus.

"How can a young man cleanse his way? By taking heed according to Your word."

* *Testimonies for the Church*, vol. 6, p. 393.

Practicing for Heaven

"The kingdom of heaven is like treasure hidden in a field, which a man found and hid;
and for joy over it he goes and sells all that he has and buys that field."
—Matthew 13:44

"How often we look upon God as our last and feeblest resource!
We go to Him because we have nowhere else to go. And then we learn
that the storms of life have driven us, not upon the rocks,
but into the desired haven."
—George MacDonald

After God called me to His side for the second time, and I responded, I again enjoyed the wonderful haven of rest in His bosom. But there were still times I was bothered by statements such as this one, referring to the saints in heaven: *"A glorious light shone all about their heads, and they were continually shouting and offering praises to God"* (*Early Writings*, p. 18). It bothered me because I was not experiencing that level of joy, nor did I feel like expressing that joy outwardly.

Have you found yourself in this same position? _____

My thinking at the time went something like this: "If I'm not praising God all the time, then maybe He isn't working in me." But I can now write to you with confidence—it was a lie of the devil! He was the one who wanted me to be depressed.

As my walk with God progressed and my love for Him grew, I found myself desiring to praise Him for many more things, but it did take time. I'm urging you to have patience with yourself because the transformation process is exactly that—a process. I grew up not showing much emotion, but over time I learned to retrain my responses to God. Praise itself has an amazing effect upon our emotions, our health, and our spiritual walk. When we praise God, we are lifted up to heavenly places.

➡ **Notice what Ellen White says regarding the educating of your tongue and heart. Underline what you must do:**

"If you sit in heavenly places with Christ, you cannot refrain from praising God. Begin to educate your tongues to praise Him and train your hearts to make melody to God; and when the evil one begins to settle his gloom about you, sing praise to God. When things go crossways at your homes, strike up a song about the matchless charms of the Son of God, and I tell you, when you touch this strain, Satan will leave you. You can drive out the enemy with his gloom; . . . and you can see, oh, so much clearer, the love and compassion of your heavenly Father" (*In Heavenly Places*, p. 95).

➡ **Now go back and circle what the response of Satan will be when you praise God.**

All this amounts to lifestyle change! As you train yourself to think upon heavenly things and lift your voice to God, the praises and testimonies that emanate from your lips will cause the devil great pain and suffering—and he will flee from you.

"They may come to their senses and escape the snare of the devil,
having been taken captive by him to do his will" (2 Tim. 2:26).

"Therefore submit to God. Resist the devil and he will flee from you. Draw near to God
and He will draw near to you. Cleanse your hands, you sinners; and purify your hearts,
you double-minded" (James 4:7, 8).

"They overcame him by the blood of the Lamb and by the word of their testimony,
and they did not love their lives to the death" (Rev. 12:11).

C. S. Lewis wrote, "Joy is the serious business of heaven." The devil wants you to be discouraged and to pass that discouragement on to others. We must train ourselves to keep looking up to our God and Savior. There we will find constant joy and happiness amid the trials of this life. Choose to be happy in Christ!

"Do not listen to Satan's lies, but recount God's promises. Gather the roses and the lilies and the pinks. Talk of the promises of God. Talk faith. Trust in God, for He is your only hope. He is my only hope. I have tremendous battles with Satan's temptations to discouragements, but I will not yield an inch. I will not give Satan an advantage over my body or my mind" (*Daughters of God*, p. 146).

"Whatever sufferings or trials you may be called upon to bear, you should not permit a breath of murmuring to escape your lips" (*Review and Herald*, Aug. 8, 1878).

➡ **Spend prayerful time thinking about those things in your life for which you can be joyful and praise God. List them here:**

- _____
- _____
- _____
- _____
- _____

➡ **Below, circle the words "praise" and "praises":**

"Oh, give thanks to the Lord, for He is good! For His mercy endures forever. And say,
'Save us, O God of our salvation; gather us together, and deliver us from the Gentiles,
to give thanks to Your holy name, to triumph in Your praise'" (1 Chron. 16:34, 35).

"Stand every morning to thank and praise the Lord, and likewise at evening"
(1 Chron. 23:30).

"Therefore by Him let us continually offer the sacrifice of praise to God, that is,
the fruit of our lips, giving thanks to His name" (Heb. 13:15).

"Rejoice in the Lord, O you righteous! For praise from the upright is beautiful"
(Ps. 33:1).

"My tongue shall speak of Your righteousness and of Your praise all the day long"
(Ps. 35:28).

"As He was now drawing near the descent of the Mount of Olives, the whole multitude of the disciples

began to rejoice and praise God with a loud voice for all the mighty works they had seen"
(Luke 19:37).

*"Whoever offers praise glorifies Me; and to him who orders his conduct aright
I will show the salvation of God" (Ps. 50:23).*

*"Then a voice came from the throne, saying, 'Praise our God, all you His servants
and those who fear Him, both small and great!' " (Rev. 19:5).*

➡ **Read *Steps to Christ*, chapter 13, "Rejoicing in the Lord."**

➡ **Taking time with the Lord.** If you are in a place where you can lift up your voice to God and are comfortable in doing so, spend some time right now openly praising Him for the blessing you wrote down earlier. In doing so, your heart will be uplifted toward heaven!

> *"The kingdom of heaven is like treasure hidden in a field,
> which a man found and hid; and for joy over it he goes
> and sells all that he has and buys that field."*

Responding to His Voice

"As many as are led by the Spirit of God, these are sons of God."
—Romans 8:14

"The true follower of Christ will not ask, 'If I embrace this truth, what will it cost me?'
Rather he will say, 'This is truth. God help me to walk in it, let come what may!'"
—A. W. Tozer

He was a young pastor in 1940 living on the island of Honshu in Sendai, Japan. The police came to his home one day and asked for Pastor Shibata. "Yes," he said, "I am he."

They said, "We have a paper that we need you to sign."

The pastor read over the paper and said, "I cannot sign this!" The document stated that Shibata believed the emperor of Japan was greater than Jesus Christ.

He would not sign, so they hauled him to the police chief—the beginning of a five-year ordeal. Accused of being a traitor, he was sent to prison. The authorities were determined to break his spirit and used every form of punishment to force him into signing. They starved him, beat him, and even pumped his stomach full of water and jumped on his belly—but nothing worked. He was steadfast in His service and devotion to the Lord!

When did he acquire the strength to resist such persecution? For years he had spent much time with the Good Shepherd and had been listening to His voice saying, "This is the way." He would have rather died than sign that paper! And dying almost became his reality. When death was staring him in the face, there was only one thing that bothered him: "Why didn't I do more for Christ when I had a chance? When I could freely walk down the street and talk to people, knock on doors, or share with souls on the train and subway, why didn't I?"

So he made a commitment to God. "Lord, if You ever let me out of this prison, I will give every ounce of my energy for Your cause." When the U.S. military arrived in Japan, he was freed from prison—and he kept his word to his King.

Will you embrace truth at any cost? If so, why? If not, why not?

"There are voices that we shall hear all around us to divert us away from the truth, but if we have an eye single to the glory of God and are striving to do His will, we shall hear . . . and know it is the voice of the Good Shepherd. It is very important that we understand the voice that speaks to us" (In Heavenly Places, p. 145).

Has God been speaking to you during this study?

☐ yes

☐ no

At the start of this workbook, in the preface, you were asked some questions. Are your answers different now than they were when you started this study? Be honest as you answer!

✓ How is your relationship with the Lord? Does He come first in everything in your life?

✓ Can you say—without a doubt—that you have been growing in your friendship with Jesus?

✓ Do you have complete assurance that if Jesus returned today, you would be excited about His return? Would you be ready to go home with Him?

✓ Is your present walk on life's pathway making Jesus happy, or are you regularly causing Him pain by yielding to every temptation?

You have been studying what it takes to hear the voice of the Good Shepherd. Select from the following list the ways in which God has spoken to you over these past 12 weeks:

☐ through Bible study
☐ through regular prayer
☐ through the Holy Spirit
☐ through circumstances
☐ through the church
☐ through the prophet of God
☐ through this study guide
☐ other: _____

How would you describe your response to the things God has asked you to do or has revealed to you? Do you have the commitment of Pastor Shibata?

_____

_____

The Lord can use all of these ways to speak to you.

A bumper sticker that was popular many years ago said, "God said it, I believe it, and that's good enough for me." I have met Christians who think this is not a good response to God, *but* it is the very response He wants you to have! When Jesus spoke, He was looking for immediate compliance.

When God speaks to you, how do you respond to Him?

☐ I argue with Him.
☐ I hesitate and question.
☐ I act immediately.
☐ I say, "Here I am, Lord."
☐ other: _____

One of the most amazing things I've witnessed while traveling the world and meeting new people is the way in which they respond to the gospel. There is a common theme that runs through most stories: From the moment they hear the voice of God calling them to *"follow Me,"* they drop everything and run into His arms. Absolutely nothing is more important to them! They immediately grasp the vision of a better world, and this life takes a back seat to following the King wherever He leads. And did I mention that they begin telling *everyone* about their newfound Friend? Why does this happen? **Because they have a childlike faith!**

"They were almost constantly with Him, witnessing His miracles, and hearing His words. John pressed into still closer intimacy with Jesus, so that he is distinguished as the one whom Jesus loved. The Savior loved them all, but John's was the most receptive spirit. He was younger than the others, and with more of the child's confiding trust he opened

his heart to Jesus. Thus he came more into sympathy with Christ, and through him the Savior's deepest spiritual teaching was communicated to His people" (*The Desire of Ages*, p. 292).

List the four attributes that allowed John to be distinguished as the one whom Jesus loved:

1. _____
2. _____
3. _____
4. _____

Do you have these attributes? _____ **If your answer is no, ask the Lord to give them to you, as they are needed in your walk with Him.**

Acts 1:8 says, *"You shall receive power when the Holy Spirit has come upon you; and you shall be witnesses to Me in Jerusalem . . . and to the end of the earth."* Jesus might ask you to go to the end of the earth to witness for Him. Are you willing? You might not be called to leave your town or state, but He is still looking for willing servants to go where He calls them!

"The cross is laid on every Christian. The first Christ-suffering which every man must experience is the call to abandon the attachments of this world. It is that dying of the old man which is the result of his encounter with Christ. As we embark upon discipleship we surrender ourselves to Christ in union with His death—we give over our lives to death. Thus it begins; the cross is not the terrible end to an otherwise godfearing and happy life, but it meets us at the beginning of our communion with Christ.

"When Christ calls a man, he bids him come and die. It may be a death like that of the first disciples who had to leave home and work to follow him, or it may be a death like Luther's, who had to leave the monastery and go out into the world. But it is the same death every time—death in Jesus Christ, the death of the old man at his call. Jesus' summons to the rich young man was calling him to die, because only the man who is dead to his own own will can follow Christ. In fact, every command of Jesus is a call to die, with all our affections and lusts" (Dietrich Bonhoeffer, *The Cost of Discipleship* [New York: Simon and Schuster, 1959], pp. 89, 90).

What is your greatest goal—your prime focus in life?

_____
_____

Your primary goal should be *to "know"* Jesus, because to know Him means *"eternal life"* (John 17:3). Listen to His voice, respond immediately, and share Him as you see God at work around you. Do this, and you will experience the most amazing transformation of character and personality!

But you might be asking, "What can God do through me? I'm so ordinary." When God is living and working in and through you, you can do anything God can do! Do you believe that? Let's see what one "ordinary" person can do for Christ . . .

- "Elijah was a man with a nature like ours" (James 5:17)—yet he brought fire down from heaven and changed a nation.
- Moses was a murderer and a mere shepherd—yet he delivered a nation from bondage.
- Abram was an old man and a liar—yet he fathered a nation.
- Peter and John were simple fishermen—yet they "rocked" the world for Christ.
- John the Baptist preached for only six months, yet Jesus said there was none greater, and he focused the world's attention upon the Lamb of God.

- Noah was the world's worst evangelist—yet he was the father of a new world.
- Lazarus was dead—yet God used him to tell of the resurrection to come.

Do you believe God can make a difference through an "ordinary" person such as you? Explain:

_____

_____

➥ **Read *Steps to Christ*, chapter 9, "The Work and the Life."**

➥ **Taking time with the Lord.** Dwight L. Moody was a simple shoe salesman when he heard Henry Varley say, "The world has yet to see what God can do with and for and through and in a man who is fully and wholly consecrated to Him." Moody was determined to become that person! The rest is history, as they say. Moody became one of the greatest soul winners the world has ever known. Ask God to give you a faith and determination like Moody had and to become a great soul winner for Him through your transformation process.

> *"As many as are led by the Spirit of God, these are sons of God."*

What a Day!

"Behold what manner of love the Father has bestowed on us, that we should be called children of God! . . . Beloved, now we are children of God; and it has not yet been revealed what we shall be, but we know that when He is revealed, we shall be like Him, for we shall see Him as He is."
—1 John 3:1, 2

Revelation 1:7 says, "Every eye will see Him." Although I have quoted a portion of a text that refers to the second coming of Christ, it holds true for His third coming as well. Yes—His third coming! After the 1,000-year reign, Christ, the redeemed, and the Holy City descend to the earth—at which time the wicked dead are raised to life. Satan will then run throughout their ranks and say to those whose numbers are like the sands of the sea, "I resurrected you! Now, you see that city? We can take it!"

Indeed, *"every eye will see Him,"* but some eyes will be standing with Christ looking out over the walls of the Celestial City, while others will be standing with the devil looking at Jesus from the outside . . . that choice is yours to make today.

Which group do you choose to be a part of?

☐ *"It will be said in that day: 'Behold, this is our God; we have waited for Him, and He will save us. This is the Lord; we have waited for Him; we will be glad and rejoice in His salvation'"* (Isa. 25:9).

☐ *"[And they] said to the mountains and rocks, 'Fall on us and hide us from the face of Him who sits on the throne and from the wrath of the Lamb! For the great day of His wrath has come, and who is able to stand?'"* (Rev. 6:16, 17).

The group referred to in Revelation asks a very testing question: "Who will be able to stand?" How would you answer them?

_____

The psalmist answered the question in Psalm 24:3-5:

"Who may ascend into the hill of the Lord? Or who may stand in His holy place? He who has clean hands and a pure heart, who has not lifted up his soul to an idol, nor sworn deceitfully. He shall receive blessing from the Lord, and righteousness from the God of his salvation."

There you have it! The ones who are happy to welcome the Mighty King at His coming are the ones who have let go of the things of this world and surrendered fully to Jesus Christ, allowing Him to purify, cleanse, and eradicate sin in their lives.

You have been learning over the course of this study that if you will release your grip on the "realities" of this world, you will find it much easier to grasp the realities of the heavenly world. You were created for eternity, and that's just what the Lord has in store for you. This world and all it contains is but a single speck of sand on the shores of forever. Your journey is not yet finished, but God has promised you a happy conclusion to this brief chapter in your life!

God gave the children of Israel a mighty promise: *"Every place that the sole of your foot will tread upon I have given you, as I said to Moses"* (Joshua 1:3). Did you notice that He had already given the Promised Land to them (past tense)? All they had to do was to believe and choose to act upon the promise.

God has done the same for you! You are a kingdom child. God is your Father, Jesus is your brother, and you are going to sit with Him on His throne for eternity! Your part is to believe it is so and to conduct yourself like the royal family member that you are.

➡ **Write your name in the blank space below**:

"To _____ who overcomes I will grant to sit with Me on My throne, as I also overcame and sat down with My Father on His throne" (Rev. 3:21).

If you are faithful, this is the group you will be a part of at the second coming of Jesus:

"We all entered the cloud together, and were seven days ascending to the sea of glass, when Jesus brought the crowns, and with His own right hand placed them on our heads" (Early Writings, p. 16).

This account is just a little glimpse of your new home—where you are going to be living:

"I saw another field full of all kinds of flowers, and as I plucked them, I cried out, 'They will never fade.' Next I saw a field of tall grass, most glorious to behold; it was living green and had a reflection of silver and gold, as it waved proudly to the glory of King Jesus. Then we entered a field full of all kinds of beasts—the lion, the lamb, the leopard, and the wolf, all together in perfect union. We passed through the midst of them, and they followed on peaceably after. Then we entered a wood, not like the dark woods we have here; no, no; but light, and all over glorious; the branches of the trees moved to and fro, and we all cried out, 'We will dwell safely in the wilderness and sleep in the woods.' We passed through the woods, for we were on our way to Mount Zion" (ibid., p. 18).

This glimpse of your new home should be etched upon your mind with laser clarity. Taste the fruit from the tree of life, smell the fragrance of the flowers, talk with the animals, and enjoy your vibrant new mind and glorious, youthful health. *God has already given it all to you—claim it as yours!* Know that it is a reality in the mind of God and will soon become your reality!

"This temple was supported by seven pillars, all of transparent gold, set with pearls most glorious. The wonderful things I there saw I cannot describe. Oh, that I could talk in the language of Canaan, then could I tell a little of the glory of the better world" (ibid., p. 19).

In the *Signs of the Times* (November 10, 1887) Ellen White refers to two classes of people in the end-times. I have taken her message and numbered it for clarity:

"Here, then, are two classes:

(1) *one seeking for the pleasures of this mortal life,*

(2) *the other for the enduring joys of immortality;*

(3) *one class are far from Christ, and satisfied with their condition,*

(4) *the other are seeking for the forgiveness of sins and for the Spirit of God;*

(5) *one class are battling against God and his truth,*

(6) *the other are warring against the lusts of the flesh, the spirit of the world, and Satan.*

(7) *One class are dreading the appearing of Christ, the Son of man, feeling that to them it is an overwhelming calamity;*

(8) *the other are looking for the coming of Christ the second time, without sin unto salvation.*

(9) *The one class will be rejected from the presence of God, and finally suffer the pangs of the second death;*

(10) *the other will have everlasting life at the right hand of God, where are pleasures forevermore."*

List the numbers of those statements that reflect your experience with Christ today:

_____

As you continue to view Jesus more clearly, grasp the joys of heaven, and seize upon the reward that awaits you, you will have the experience described by Ellen White after she returned from heaven to earth via a remarkable vision:

> "After I came out of vision, everything looked changed; a gloom was spread over all that I beheld. Oh, how dark this world looked to me. I wept when I found myself here, and felt homesick. I had seen a better world, and it had spoiled this for me" (Early Writings, p. 20).

Select the statement(s) that best reflects your heart:

☐ There is nothing in this world that holds an attraction for me any longer.

☐ I love Jesus with all of my heart and choose to follow Him.

☐ I praise Him for His love and power to enable me to walk in His pathway.

☐ I choose to join Him in His work so the world can hear the good news.

☐ I am reaching higher each day.

☐ other: _____

➥ **Write your name in each blank space below:**

> "God grant . . . that when Jesus shall come the second time, _____ may be found ready and waiting; that _____ may be of that number who shall sing the song of redemption around the great white throne, casting their crowns at the feet of the redeemer. God grant that, with all the redeemed, _____ may have the glorious privilege of standing upon the sea of glass and walking the streets of gold. God grant that at that time there may be given to _____ hand a harp of gold, and that as _____ sweep its strings all Heaven may resound with _____ notes of joy and praise" (Signs of the Times, Nov. 10, 1887).

➥ **Read Steps to Christ, chapter 2, "The Sinner's Need of Christ."**

➥ **Taking time with the Lord.** Go to God in thanksgiving and let this be your prayer: "The Spirit Himself bears witness with our spirit that we are children of God, and if children, then heirs—heirs of God and joint heirs with Christ, if indeed we suffer with Him, that we may also be glorified together. For I consider that the sufferings of this present time are not worthy to be compared with the glory which shall be revealed in us" (Rom. 8:16-18). Rejoice in prayer that you are in the process of being transformed into the likeness of Jesus Christ, our Lord!

*****

It is my prayer that this past 12 weeks of _Your Daily Journey to Transformation_ study has become the launching pad for the most exciting journey of your life—one that will continue throughout eternity. I am looking forward to meeting you at the feet of our Lord very soon!

Quotes to Lead You Higher Still

The following verse lies at the very center of the Bible:

"It is better to trust in the Lord than to put confidence in man" (Ps. 118:8).

"There is no peace in the border lands. The halfway Christian is a torment to himself and of no benefit to others" (Earnest Worker).

"You need not go to the ends of the earth for wisdom, for God is near. It is not the capabilities you now possess or ever will have that will give you success. It is that which the Lord can do for you. We need to have far less confidence in what man can do and far more confidence in what God can do for every believing soul. He longs to have you reach after Him by faith. He longs to have you expect great things from Him. He longs to give you understanding in temporal as well as in spiritual matters. He can sharpen the intellect. He can give tact and skill. Put your talents into the work, ask God for wisdom, and it will be given you" (Christ's Object Lessons, p. 146).

"Courage, fortitude, faith, and implicit trust in God's power to save, do not come in a moment. These heavenly graces are acquired by the experience of years. By a life of holy endeavor and firm adherence to the right, the children of God were sealing their destiny" (Christian Experience and Teachings of Ellen G. White, p. 188).

"In his own strength man cannot rule his spirit. But through Christ he may gain self-control. In His strength he may bring his thoughts and words into subjection to the will of God. The religion of Christ brings the emotions under the control of reason and disciplines the tongue. Under its influence the hasty temper is subdued, and the heart is filled with patience and gentleness" (Messages to Young People, p. 136).

"Hold firmly to the One who has all power in heaven and in earth. Though you so often fail to reveal patience and calmness, do not give up the struggle. Resolve again, this time more firmly, to be patient under every provocation. And never take your eyes off your divine Example" (Review and Herald, Oct. 31, 1907).

"We may grow as the lily, revive as the corn, and grow as the vine. By constantly looking to and patterning after Christ, as our personal Savior, we shall grow up into Him in all things. Our faith will grow, our conscience will be sanctified. We will more and more become like Christ in all our works and words" (Manuscript Releases, vol. 4, p. 356).

"When God gave His Son to the world, He made it possible for men and women to be perfect by the use of every capability of their beings to the glory of God. In Christ He gave to them the riches of His grace, and a knowledge of His will. As they would empty themselves of self, and learn to walk in humility, leaning on God for guidance, men would be enabled to fulfill God's high purpose for them.

"*Perfection of character is based upon that which Christ is to us. If we have constant dependence on the merits of our Savior, and walk in His footsteps, we shall be like Him, pure and undefiled.*

"*Our Savior does not require impossibilities of any soul. He expects nothing of His disciples that He is not willing to give them grace and strength to perform. He would not call upon them to be perfect if He had not at His command every perfection of grace to bestow on the ones upon whom He would confer so high and holy a privilege. . . .*

"*Our Savior is a Savior for the perfection of the whole man. He is not the God of part of the being only. The grace of Christ works to the disciplining of the whole human fabric. He made all. He has redeemed all. He has made the mind, the strength, the body as well as the soul, partaker of the divine nature, and all is His purchased possession. He must be served with the whole mind, heart, soul, and strength. Then the Lord will be glorified in His saints in even the common, temporal things with which they are connected. 'Holiness unto the Lord' will be in the inscription placed upon them*" (*Our Father Cares*, p. 214).

"*Christ tells us not to be worried nor afraid, but to remember what He can do if we come to Him, trusting in His strength. He says, If you yoke up with Me, your Redeemer, I will be your strength, your efficiency*" (*Review and Herald*, Oct. 23, 1900).

Ellen G. White Sources

The Acts of the Apostles (Mountain View, Calif.: Pacific Press Pub. Assn., 1911), pp. 50, 54, 55, 476.

The Adventist Home (Washington, D.C.: Review and Herald Pub. Assn., 1952), pp. 54, 331, 546, 548.

An Appeal to the Youth (Battle Creek, Mich.: Seventh-day Adventist Pub. Assn., 1864), p. 70.

The Bible Echo, Oct. 15, 1900.

Child Guidance (Washington, D.C.: Review and Herald Pub. Assn., 1954), p. 209.

Christ Triumphant (Hagerstown, Md.: Review and Herald Pub. Assn., 1999), p. 289.

Christian Experience and Teachings of Ellen G. White (Mountain View, Calif.: Pacific Press Pub. Assn., 1922), p. 188.

Christian Service (Washington, D.C.: Review and Herald Pub. Assn., 1925), p. 41.

Christ's Object Lessons (Washington, D.C.: Review and Herald Pub. Assn., 1900), pp. 18, 19, 96, 116, 118, 121, 146, 333, 355.

Counsels for the Church (Nampa, Idaho: Pacific Press Pub. Assn., 1991), pp. 98, 99.

Counsels on Health (Mountain View, Calif.: Pacific Press Pub. Assn., 1923), pp. 108, 598.

Daughters of God (Hagerstown, Md.: Review and Herald Pub. Assn., 1998), p. 146.

The Desire of Ages (Mountain View, Calif.: Pacific Press Pub. Assn., 1898), pp. 256, 292, 311, 530.

Early Writings (Washington, D.C.: Review and Herald Pub. Assn., 1882, 1945), pp. 16-20, 64.

The Faith I Live By (Washington, D.C.: Review and Herald Pub. Assn., 1958), pp. 125, 332.

Fundamentals of Christian Education (Nashville: Southern Pub. Assn., 1923), p. 126.

Gospel Workers (Washington, D.C.: Review and Herald Pub. Assn., 1915), p. 246.

In Heavenly Places (Washington, D.C.: Review and Herald Pub. Assn., 1967), pp. 21, 95, 145, 170, 190, 298.

Lift Him Up (Hagerstown, Md.: Review and Herald Pub. Assn., 1988), pp. 65, 360.

Loma Linda Messages (Payson, Ariz.: Leaves of Autumn Books, 1981), p. 33.

Manuscript Releases (Silver Spring, Md.: Ellen G. White Estate, 1981, 1987, 1990, 1993), vol. 3, p. 434; vol. 4, p. 356; vol. 5, p. 368; vol. 14, pp. 27, 28.

Medical Ministry (Mountain View, Calif.: Pacific Press Pub. Assn., 1932), p. 244.

Messages to Young People (Washington, D.C.: Review and Herald Pub. Assn., 1930), pp. 81, 136.

Mind, Character, and Personality (Nashville: Southern Pub. Assn., 1977), vol. 1, p. 324.

The Ministry of Healing (Mountain View, Calif.: Pacific Press Pub. Assn., 1905), pp. 94, 176.

My Life Today (Washington, D.C.: Review and Herald Pub. Assn., 1952), pp. 283, 318.

Our Father Cares (Hagerstown, Md.: Review and Herald Pub. Assn., 1991), pp. 134, 214.

Review and Herald, July 21, 1851; May 31, 1870; Aug. 8, 1878; Jan. 19, 1886; Mar. 19, 1889; Feb. 5, 1895; June 18, 1895; Nov. 12, 1895; June 23, 1896; Aug. 4, 1896; Oct. 5, 1897; Oct. 23, 1900; Oct. 31, 1907; May 28, 1908; July 4, 1912.

Selected Messages (Washington, D.C.: Review and Herald Pub. Assn., 1958, 1980), book 1, p. 346; book 2, p. 374; book 3, p. 114.

Sermons and Talks (Silver Spring, Md.: Ellen G. White Estate, 1990, 1994), vol. 1, p. 285.

The Seventh-day Adventist Bible Commentary, Ellen G. White Comments (Washington, D.C.: Review and Herald Pub. Assn., 1953-1957), vol. 7, p. 908.

Signs of the Times, June 12, 1901; May 18, 1904; Apr. 12, 1905.

Sons and Daughters of God (Washington, D.C.: Review and Herald Pub. Assn., 1955), p. 7.

Steps to Christ (Mountain View, Calif.: Pacific Press Pub. Assn., 1956), pp. 22, 93, 94.

Testimonies for the Church (Mountain View, Calif.: Pacific Press Pub. Assn., 1948), vol. 2, p. 608; vol. 4, p. 251; vol. 5, p. 590; vol. 6, p. 393; vol. 8, pp. 186, 187.

Testimonies to Southern Africa (Cape Town: South African Union Conference of Seventh-day Adventists, 1977), p. 30.

The Upward Look (Washington, D.C.: Review and Herald Pub. Assn., 1982), p. 322.

Youth's Instructor, Jan. 3, 1895; Sept. 9, 1897; Feb. 1, 1900; Oct. 3, 1901.

They Didn't Believe in Jesus.

He Showed Up Anyway.

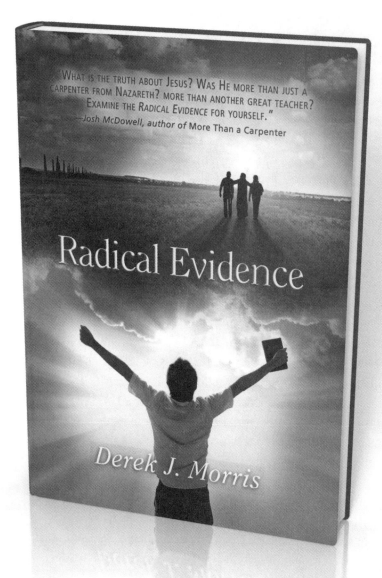

"WHAT IS THE TRUTH ABOUT JESUS? WAS HE MORE THAN JUST A CARPENTER FROM NAZARETH? MORE THAN ANOTHER GREAT TEACHER? EXAMINE THE RADICAL EVIDENCE FOR YOURSELF."
—Josh McDowell, author of More Than a Carpenter

Radical Evidence

Derek J. Morris

In his latest book, Derek Morris introduces you to people who have had a dramatic encounter with the Messiah they didn't believe in. There's a Shiite Muslim and an African ancestor worshipper. There's Clifford Goldstein, an atheist and obsessed novelist who found his life taking an unexpected turn.

People in Bible times also present evidence. There are the prophets who spoke of things they did not understand, but whose words came true in the gospel story.

Perhaps you have a friend who has doubts about the divinity of Jesus. Or maybe you work with a straight-up unbeliever. Invite them to read this book and see the radical evidence for a real and personal Savior.

Hardcover: 978-0-8127-0514-0. **US$11.99**

DVD: Four presentations, approx. 28 minutes each. 978-1-936929-07-8. **US$9.95**

eBOOK AVAILABLE

Other books in the Radical series you may enjoy

The Radical Prayer

Hardcover: 978-0-8127-0486-0. US$10.99

Audio CD: 978-0-981712-41-3. US$8.95

DVD: 978-0-981712-40-6. **US$9.95**

Spanish: Paperback: 978-8-472082-67-0. **US$5.99**

Radical Protection

Hardcover: 978-0-8127-0476-1. US$11.99

Audio CD: 978-1-936929-01-6. US$9.95

DVD: 978-1-936929-00-9. **US$9.95**

Trilogy Scripture Songs CD: 978-1-936929-02-3. **US$9.95**

The Radical Teachings of Jesus

Hardcover: 978-0-8127-0498-3. US$11.99

Audio CD: 978-0-981712-49-9. US$8.95

DVD: 978-0-981712-42-0. **US$9.95**

Leader's Kit: 978-1-932267-77-8. US$49.95

Prices and availability subject to change. Sale prices in effect through August 31, 2013. Canadian prices higher.

This Could Change Everything.

Find transforming power for your life.

Do you feel like temptations always beat you into submission? You can't seem to win a victory and wonder if you're not trying hard enough, or if God isn't holding up His end of the bargain.

In the book *Transformation* Jim Ayer opens up about his own experience as a serial sinner and tells how he connected with the power that God has provided to change us from the inside out.

Read this book to begin an exciting lifelong journey. "Behold, I make all things new," says the Lord. See that promise fulfilled in your life today.

Transformation
"Behold, I make all things new"
Jim Ayer
978-0-8280-2711-3

Remodeling Your Life
God's Transforming Power
Jim Ayer
Twelve 30-minute television episodes on three DVDs.
978-0-8280-2702-1

Availability subject to change.

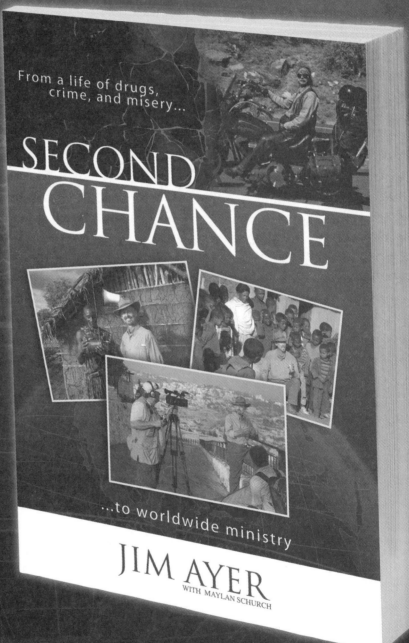